Environmental Comm
Among Minority Popu

C000146072

There are many current socio-environmental conflicts and problems around the world that affect distinct nationalities, races, or ethnicities. Part of the solution to these issues involves interdisciplinary scholarship to make sense of the communication challenges that are involved. However, current research in this area has lacked clear focus on the ways in which environmental issues are culturally and socially constructed by racial and ethnic minorities.

This volume aims to improve our understanding of culturally bounded rationalities across racial and ethnic groups facing environmental challenges, as they relate to the formation of environmental identities, environmental injustice, political activism, public engagement, and media representations, among others. The ideas presented in this book dovetail with the idea that environmental communication scholars and practitioners can effectively intervene to engage ethnic groups that traditionally are not included in decision-making or deliberation processes that directly affect their livelihoods.

Considering problems such as the siting of industrial facilities, flooding, droughts, climate change, and air and water pollution, this book will be of great interest to students, scholars, and practitioners of environmental communication.

Bruno Takahashi is Research Director and Associate Professor at the Knight Center for Environmental Journalism, Michigan State University, USA.

Sonny Rosenthal is Assistant Professor at the Wee Kim Wee School of Communication and Information, Nanyang Technological University, Singapore.

Routledge Focus on Environment and Sustainability

For more information about this series, please visit: www.routledge.com/ Routledge-Focus-on-Environment-and-Sustainability/book-series/RFES

Environmental Communication Among Minority Populations

Edited by Bruno Takahashi and
Sonny Rosenthal

LONDON AND NEW YORK

First published 2019
by Routledge

2 Park Square, Milton Park, Abingdon, Oxfordshire OX14 4RN
52 Vanderbilt Avenue, New York, NY 10017

Routledge is an imprint of the Taylor & Francis Group, an informa business

First issued in paperback 2020

British Library Cataloguing-in-Publication Data
A catalogue record for this book is available from the British Library

Library of Congress Cataloging-in-Publication Data
A catalog record for this book has been requested

ISBN: 978-0-8153-5684-4 (hbk)
ISBN: 978-0-367-60669-5 (pbk)

Typeset in Times New Roman
by Apex CoVantage, LLC

Contents

Figures

Table

Contributors

B.F. Battistoli is an assistant professor of journalism at Fairleigh Dickinson University. His primary area of research is risk communication, with a particular focus on minority and disadvantaged populations at risk from natural disasters.

Mohan J. Dutta, Ph.D., is Provost's Chair Professor and Head of the Department of Communications and New Media at the National University of Singapore. He is the founding director of the Center for Culture-Centered Approach to Research and Evaluation (CARE). His research examines the meanings of health among marginalized communities and ways in which participatory culture-centered processes and strategies are organized for social change.

Maria Knight Lapinski is a professor in the Department of Communication and Michigan AgBio Research at Michigan State University. She is director of the College of Communication Arts and Science's Health and Risk Communication Center. She studies the role of cultural dynamics and interpersonal influence in health, environment, and risk communication.

Rain Wuyu Liu, Ph.D., is an assistant professor in the School of Communication at Bellarmine University. Her research interests include interpersonal communication, persuasion, intercultural communication, and social influence. Specifically, her research focuses on the impacts of social norms on health and environment information processing, attitude change, and health and conservation behavior promotion.

Jessica Love-Nichols is a Ph.D. candidate in linguistics at the University of California, Santa Barbara with an interdepartmental Ph.D. emphasis in Environment and Society. Her research interests include language, identity, environmental ideologies, and conservation practices in rural Nicaragua and the United States. Before starting her graduate studies in linguistics, Jessica served for three years as an Environmental Education Volunteer with the Peace Corps in Nicaragua.

Patrick D. Murphy, Ph.D., Ohio University, is Associate Dean for Research and Graduate Studies at Temple University's Klein College of Media and Communication. His teaching and research interests include media and globalization, media and the environment, ethnographic method, and Latin American media and cultural theory.

Clemencia Rodríguez is a professor in the Department of Media Studies and Production at Temple University's Klein College of Media and Communication. Her research explores media appropriation processes by communities and social movements. In her book *Fissures in the Mediascape: An International Study of Citizens' Media* (2001), Rodríguez developed her "citizens' media theory," a ground-breaking approach to understanding the role of community/alternative media in our societies.

Sonny Rosenthal, Ph.D., The University of Texas at Austin, is an assistant professor in the Wee Kim Wee School of Communication and Information at Nanyang Technological University, Singapore. His main research focus is climate change communication, in which he studies public opinion, social marketing strategy, and effects of narratives. Other areas of research interest include the third-person effect and quantitative methodology.

Kami Silk, Ph.D., is a professor of communication and Chair of the Department of Communication at the University of Delaware. Her research interests are in the areas of health communication and persuasion with a particular focus on translational research on environmental exposures and breast cancer risk. Dr. Silk has also engaged in environmental communication research related to the bioeconomy in Michigan, the impact of vermiculite in Montana on residents, and the Flint water crisis.

Bruno Takahashi, Ph.D., SUNY ESF, is an associate professor of environmental journalism and communication at Michigan State University. Dr. Takahashi is also the research director of the Knight Center of Environmental Journalism. He is the past chair of the Environmental Communication Division of the International Communication Association. His research interests include media coverage of environmental affairs, environmental journalism practices, risk communication, and the links between media and policy.

Jagadish Thaker, Ph.D., is a senior lecturer at the School of Communication, Journalism and Marketing at Massey University, New Zealand. His research examines ways to understand and enhance vulnerable communities' adaptive capacity to climate change impacts, and he specializes in the fields of science and climate change communication, health communication, and strategic communication campaigns.

Daniel Totzkay, M.A., is a doctoral candidate in the Department of Communication at Michigan State University. His research interests include formative evaluation for risk reduction and health promotion campaigns, persuasive message design, and translating communication theory to applied contexts.

Amanda Williams is an adjunct associate professor for the Faculty of Business and Communication Studies at Mount Royal University in Calgary, Alberta. Her current research interests include explorations of discourses of sustainability in regards to the Alberta Oil Sands and systems of entrepreneurship.

Acknowledgments

The Editors would like to thank the participants of the pre-conference *Communicating environmental issues among racial/ethnic minorities* that was held at the 67th Annual Conference of the International Communication Association in San Diego, CA. This book was only possible thanks to their participation and input. We would also like to acknowledge the support of our institutions, the College of Communication Arts and Sciences at Michigan State University, and the Wee Kim Wee School of Communication and Information at Nanyang Technological University.

Introduction

Bruno Takahashi and Sonny Rosenthal

People's understandings of nature and environmental problems are culturally grounded (Macias, 2015; Schultz, 2002). However, research in environmental communication still requires the development of robust models or frameworks to help researchers design projects that not only account for culture, but that incorporate culture within the core of research and communication designs (Anderson, 2015). In the introduction to this edited volume, we explore the limitations in environmental communication and present six chapters that address those challenges.

The aim of this edited volume is two-fold. First, it seeks to highlight current and future scholarship at the intersection of race and ethnic studies and environmental communication. Second, it seeks to address the spectrum of issues at this intersection by applying diverse international perspectives, methods, and subfields within communication and related disciplines.

There are many socio-environmental conflicts and problems around the world that affect distinct nationalities, races, or ethnicities (e.g., Levy & Patz, 2015). Part of the solution to these issues involves interdisciplinary scholarship to make sense of the communication challenges that are involved. However, current research in this area has lacked clear focus on the ways in which environmental issues are socially constructed by racial and ethnic minorities. Many of these environmental problems, including but not limited to the siting of industrial facilities, flooding, droughts, climate change, and air and water pollution disproportionately affect minority populations.

These issues are also important for international communication scholars. Racial and ethnic groups define nature and environmental protection differently. As a result, these definitions affect environmental laws and policies through their influence on public knowledge, political culture, institutions, and subjective human perceptions. Therefore, an examination of the cultural characteristics of different racial and ethnic publics is relevant to how environmental protection takes shape. Conversely, questions about the meaning of sustainability and environmentalism are relevant to how individuals construct their ethnic identities.

This edited book seeks to improve our understanding of culturally bounded rationalities across racial and ethnic groups facing environmental challenges, as they relate to the formation of environmental identities, environmental injustice, political activism, public engagement, and media representations, among others. This book fits with the idea that environmental communication scholars and practitioners can effectively intervene to engage ethnic groups that traditionally are not included in decision-making or deliberation processes that directly affect their livelihoods (Swim & Bloodhart, 2018). We hope to pave the way for additional prospective research on these topics.

This edited volume developed from the pre-conference *Communicating environmental issues among racial/ethnic minorities* organized by the co-editors at the 67th Annual Conference of the International Communication Association in San Diego, CA. The pre-conference was a first step into trying to more firmly position the concepts of race and ethnicity within the environmental communication scholarship presented at the conference. This edited book seeks to expand such discussion into the international arena of environmental communication scholarship.

In Chapter 1, Lapinski, Silk, Liu, and Totzkay present two cases that clarify aspects of communicating with unique populations. The cases demonstrate different approaches to engaging with communities and incorporating community insights into communication interventions. The first case is a program by the Breast Cancer and the Environment Research Center, which links scientists from different disciplines to understand environmental risk factors associated with breast cancer. Key team members are communication scientists, who support community engagement, conduct audience analysis, and develop communication materials, among other important activities. The second case is the Financial Incentives in Normative Systems research project, which examines the use of incentives to offset the financial costs of environmental conservation behaviors in Tibet. The program involves collaboration between international and local researchers. The two cases differ conceptually with respect to their regional scope, level of community participation, and complexity of structure. Yet they are similar in their community capacity building, shared decision-making, and transdisciplinarity. The chapter situates these differences and similarities in relation to broader models of community-engaged communication with unique populations. The discussion contains insights for researchers and practitioners proposing or embarking on large-scale environmental communication projects.

In Chapter 2, Battistoli traces, in the context of climate change, the arc of race as a factor in the risk communication process, the growing attention to socioeconomic status, and the resultant implications for risk communication research and practice. One challenge facing the communication of risk to racial minorities is that racial divides complicate the delivery and reception of information campaigns. Nonetheless, recent work on risk communication has treated race not as a primary determinant in the communication process, but rather as one of many demographic variables used to describe message audiences. Simultaneously, socioeconomic status has become an increasingly important factor in research about risk communication. Battistoli calls in this chapter for a stronger focus not only on demographic factors, but also on geographic determinants and the capacity of individuals and social groups to adapt to environmental challenges.

In Chapter 3, Murphy and Rodríguez draw from the participatory models of communication for social change and environmental communication to explore the functions of green radicalism and participatory media in the context of a digital media intervention to encourage children and youth to participate in local green initiatives in Philadelphia. The city has developed a number of community environmental initiatives, including collective gardens, urban agriculture, and composting facilities. However, these initiatives engage mostly older citizens. Local youth rarely engage with the creation and maintenance of green spaces in their local neighborhoods or are given a voice in the process. The goal of *Urban Green Spaces* is to use media and digital technologies to connect urban youth to local green spaces in Philadelphia's low-income communities, which are primarily black and Latino. Rodríguez and Murphy, who are involved in the project, explore its intended outcomes. These outcomes include increased youth engagement with urban green spaces and greater awareness of environmental justice issues such as sustainability, food security, climate change, and the significance of green spaces in urban environments among local youth.

In Chapter 4, Williams explores the meaning of "sustainability" in relation to the Alberta oil sands. This meaning arises in discussions among stakeholders, which businesses, non-profits, and government voices tend to dominate, sometimes to the exclusion of Indigenous voices. Williams takes a unique approach to studying this issue, examining the metaphors that stakeholders use to define sustainability in terms of social, economic, and environmental outcomes. These definitions can strategically reframe the issue and draw the focus of subsequent conversations. Williams highlights this use of metaphors and considers the variety and depth of metaphors that stakeholders employ and to what extent they engage the perspectives of Indigenous groups. Her qualitative analysis of 159 documents from government, NGOs, industry, and media sources reveal that metaphors are plentiful and diverse, but tend to give superficial or incomplete definitions of sustainability and largely ignore the views of Indigenous groups. Her discussion offers some critical insights about the limitations and potential avenues of using metaphors to communicate about sustainability, emphasizing the role of local knowledge inherent in Indigenous perspectives.

In Chapter 5, Love-Nichols presents findings from ethnographic field work from a central Nicaraguan community and analysis of interviews and governmental environmental campaigns. These research efforts examined the role of environmental values as predictors of pro-environmental behaviors. Love-Nichols argues that although researchers have begun to examine how these values may differ across racial and ethnic groups, less is known about how cultural differences might affect environmental communication among those audiences. The analyses suggest that environmental communication can benefit from ethnographic and discourse analytic methodologies, which can clarify how environmental values are situated within locally relevant frameworks of values and identities. Further, she argues that in Nicaragua, environmental values exist in an inseparable bundle with other cultural values, such as an orientation to public health, respect for institutions, and the hygiene of public and private spaces.

In Chapter 6, Thaker and Dutta explore the co-construction of "climate change" and "adaptation" among minority women farmers in India. The authors argue that technological approaches to climate change adaptation, such as genetically modified crops, can disrupt existing adaptive strategies among local population groups. Dominant portrayals of climate change present it as a science and engineering problem and divorce it from social and cultural contexts. Such portrayals may conflict with adaptation strategies based on local knowledge. Further, disempowering metaphors about women in the global South delegitimize their independent efforts to cope with climate change. Even when there are local-level climate change solutions, they often underserve women. The authors present the results of a study that interviewed Dalit women farmers to understand climate change and adaptation from their perspectives. The results contrast local knowledge and practices with top-down efforts to implement technological solutions. Key themes address environmental change, adaptation strategies, women in adaptation, farmer independence, and adaptation policies. These themes broach social, economic, and environmental aspects of sustainability, making a strong case that top-down approaches have limited import, particularly for underserved minority groups. The discussion resonates with a large body of literature that promotes a participatory approach to scientific and environmental issues.

In summary, the chapters in this edited book highlight the challenges of environmental communication research in relation to racial and ethnic cultural norms and artifacts in each specific context. These challenges include, among others, ignoring the cultural context by applying one's own cultural lens to the research; applying theoretical frameworks and concepts grounded in different cultural realities; and making assumptions about what communities need or want in regards to environmental matters. On the other hand, the chapters highlight some suggested practices to avoid such pitfalls, including the importance of interdisciplinary research collaborations not only across disciplines, but also across cultures. This might also include a stronger emphasis on participatory research that incorporates research subjects into the different stages of research projects. Another suggestion is to spend more time in the field with the communities to have a better understanding of their context and avoid engaging in parachute research practices. We hope this edited book will contribute to the development of robust and culturally sensitive environmental communicating research.

References

Anderson, A. (2015). Reflections on environmental communication and the challenges of a new research agenda. *Environmental Communication, 9*(3), 379–383. doi:10.1080/17524032.2015.1044063

Levy, B. S., & Patz, J. A. (2015). Climate change, human rights, and social justice. *Annals of Global Health, 81*(3), 310–322. doi:10.1016/j.aogh.2015.08.008

Macias, T. (2015). Environmental risk perception among race and ethnic groups in the United States. *Ethnicities, 16*(1), 111–129. doi:10.1177/1468796815575382

Schultz, W. P. (2002). Environmental attitudes and behaviors across cultures. *Online Readings in Psychology and Culture, 8*(1). doi:10.9707/2307-0919.1070

Swim, J. K., & Bloodhart, B. (2018). The intergroup foundations of climate change justice. *Group Processes & Intergroup Relations, 21*(3), 472–496. doi:10.1177/1368430217745366

1 Models for environmental communication for unique populations

Cases from the field

Maria Knight Lapinski, Kami Silk,
Rain Wuyu Liu and Daniel Totzkay

Introduction

Models for large-scale health communication efforts to engage unique populations are common (e.g., CDCP Effective Interventions, 2017); yet these models are seen less often in environmental communication efforts. This chapter reports results and continuing activities of two programs of environmental communication scholarship that involve partnerships with communities to engage in research, outreach, and dissemination activities. Specifically, the Breast Cancer and Environment Research Program (BCERP) and the Financial Incentives in Normative Systems (FINS) research program are discussed. The chapter then compares the two community-based approaches and identifies lessons learned that can inform the design of related environmental communication research efforts. It also highlights future opportunities for research and communication activities as these programs continue. The chapter focuses particularly on the approaches these programs have taken to engage unique communities in the research and design process as well as the ways in which the programs have translated research findings into practice.

In using the term *unique*, it is meant that these communities function at the margins of society (co-cultural groups, Orbe, 1998) or are different from a dominant cultural group. These groups or communities can be characterized based on shared linguistic features, psychological states, values, and belief systems that separate them from some dominant group within a nation state or geographical boundary. By considering groups based on shared cultural characteristics and identities, we intentionally avoid using the term minority because it is a label that implies a numerical category. The two programs presented here focus on populations with distinct needs, patterns of cognition, and preferences for communication that are crucial to consider for effective intervention design. One case involves moving community insights and social research into the design and dissemination of environmental communication efforts; the other involves using community-engaged research to inform the design and dissemination of environmental policies. First, it is useful to describe the nature of transdisciplinary, community-engaged communication research for unique populations.

Transdisciplinary, community-engaged research and design

A common thread of the BCERP and FINS are that both programs involve community-engaged design of the research and intervention activities. Community-engaged design, although a relatively new label for communication research and practice (Neuhauser, Kreps, & Syme, 2014), is an old concept. Engaging communities in communication research and intervention design is described in foundational approaches to communication study. As far back as *The Rhetoric*, Aristotle wrote extensively on the need for a speaker to understand the values and characteristics of audiences in order to be a persuasive and engaging speaker, identifying the importance of interactivity and engagement. Basic communication campaign design courses focus on stages at which a campaign"s focal community is brought into the design process. For example, Rice and Atkin's (2012) foundational text describes the ways in which effective communication campaigns involve audiences (or communities) in the design, creation, and refinement of communication efforts through the use of needs assessment, formative evaluation, assessment of the communication environment, and other processes for bringing community voices to the table. Such activities suggest the role of community members ranges from little or no community engagement with professionally designed messages and campaign materials to extensive engagement, wherein the community sets research priorities and inputs directly on intervention design.

Cases where there is limited engagement may include models where a communication campaign, program of research, or intervention is designed and implemented by a team of experts, independent of input from community members. This is a common approach when experts believe they have a strong understanding of their target audience(s) and have a specific, evidence-based message they deem as clear and necessary to communicate (e.g., Smokey the Bear; The Ad Council, 2017). At the other end of the engagement continuum sits community-based participatory research (CBPR) approaches where community members may drive decisions about the focal issues, populations, and problems for interventions or the hypotheses and research questions under study (c.f., Oetzel, Simpson, Berryman, Iti, & Reddy, 2015). For example, the HIV/AIDS Prevention Community Planning in the United States where members of the HIV positive community and unique populations disproportionately impacted by HIV/ AIDS (e.g., men who have sex with men; commercial sex workers) identified priority research areas, set intervention priorities, and helped to craft and disseminate communication interventions (c.f., Lapinski, Randall, Peterson, Peterson, & Klein, 2009).

Finally, there are many programs and projects in the middle of the continuum, in which community members are engaged at a variety of levels including as key informants, providing data on community needs, leading the design of communication materials, or actually implementing the intervention itself.

Community-engaged communication design and research, by definition, accounts for the characteristics of unique population groups. Again, the term "unique populations" is used in this case to include groups that function at the margins of society (co-cultural groups; Orbe, 1998) or that can be juxtaposed with a dominant cultural group. Co-cultural groups share a set of meanings relative to those held by a larger system (Orbe, 1998); that is, social communities exhibiting shared, learned communication characteristics, perceptions, values, beliefs, and practices. When examining communication patterns and practices, identifying groups based on shared meanings and psycho-social characteristics is more useful and insightful than classifying people based on simple demographics like race or ethnicity. Indeed, identification of these shared meanings, values, behaviors, and attitudes is fundamental to community-engaged design and research. Thus, more effective programming around a problem can arise from applying this inclusive approach to intervention design and team planning.

When addressing multifaceted societal issues, the use of a transdisciplinary model is necessary. Transdisciplinary team science is founded on the assumption that some problems are so large and complex that in order to address them, multiple disciplines need to come together. Transdisciplinary research involves diverse teams designing innovations through research and outreach efforts that transcend traditional disciplinary approaches to a problem. These innovations may be conceptual, theoretical, methodological, or translational mechanisms created by the team to address a common challenge (Harvard School of Public Health, 2012). The transdisciplinary research model focuses on translating research findings into practice; this ensures the state of the science is communicated beyond academic journals so that interventions and communication efforts are informed by the most recent scientific findings (Silk & Smith, 2016; Stokols, 2006). Transdisciplinary teams are organized to be inclusive of not only researchers from different disciplines, but also members of relevant communities, including people focused on a specific environmental issue. Transdisciplinary teams are comprised of team members from academic institutions and community organizations to create partnerships and networks consisting of the necessary areas of expertise to accomplish research or intervention goals. Transdisciplinary research is distinct from more familiar orientations like interdisciplinary and multidisciplinary research (Mitchell, 2005). Interdisciplinary research involves not just combining or juxtaposing concepts and methods from different fields but integrating divergent perspectives to create something new. Multidisciplinary research, on the other hand, emphasizes working sequentially or independently and then coming together at the late stages of research. Transdisciplinary research models, however, integrate perspectives across disciplines in order to create new approaches, paradigms, and methods to address a research problem that would not have been realized by independent and separated research initiatives undertaken in distinct disciplines (Kreps & Maibach, 2008) akin to *third culture building* in the intercultural communication literature.

Research on the "science of team science" holds lessons for the ways in which effective teams function (e.g., Falk-Krzesinski et al., 2011; O'Rourke & Crowley, 2013). Below we present two cases of community-engaged, transdisciplinary environmental communication efforts. For each program, we describe the program activities and outcomes, the nature of the team including mechanisms for community engagement, and the ways in which the program findings and processes are moved into practice. These programs address two very different issues; the first case is focused on communication about environmental risks for breast cancer, while the second case examines the role of communication in environmentally focused economic policies.

Case 1: breast cancer and the environment research center

The first program that includes a unique population in the development and implementation of communication interventions is the BCERP, funded initially by the National Institutes of Environmental Health Sciences (NIEHS) and the National Cancer Institute (NCI) beginning in 2003, and with current funding awarded through 2020. The BCERP partners communication scientists with biologists, epidemiologists, and community advocates to investigate the role of environmental risk factors in breast cancer. The BCERP is particularly interested in different "windows of susceptibility" such as puberty and pregnancy because females are more vulnerable to environmental exposures during these time periods, which can increase breast cancer risk. Another primary goal of the BCERP is to support risk reduction efforts through community engagement and strategic communication endeavors. The BCERP is organized around three cores: 1) Biology; 2) Epidemiology; and 3) Communication, Outreach, and Dissemination (COD). Each of these cores collaborates with the others on specific projects and through working group structures designed to facilitate transdisciplinary research. Each of these cores is represented by a number of institutions and community partners across the United States, all of which are tied to a central coordinating center (see Figure 1.1) in Madison, WI. These institutions are those primarily funded through the overarching BCERP mechanisms, with other institutions, researchers, and community partners connected to these larger institutions. These funded institutions include Michigan State University (MSU) (East Lansing, MI), Silent Spring Institute (Newton, MA), the University of Massachusetts, Amherst (Amherst, MA), Columbia University (New York, NY), the City of Hope National Medical Center (Duarte, CA), and Georgetown University (Washington, DC). Each funded institution is required to have a COD core, which makes community partnerships an essential feature of the organizational structure and function of the research projects.

A primary goal of the BCERP is for researchers across disciplines to communicate regularly with each other so that new evidence is more quickly shared among them and then translated for lay public consumption. Specifically, the BCERP is concerned with the perceptions and preferences of women, especially mothers with young daughters. This unique population has distinct concerns, especially for their children, and reacts to breast cancer risk reduction information differently based on maternal appeals of responsibility (e.g., Neuberger, Silk, Yun, Bowman, & Anderson, 2011). A chief concern of the BCERP is to include the opinions and views of breast cancer community advocates in the overall functioning and decision-making of the organization, in addition to the research agendas of the scientists within the group. Engaging community advocates as a unique population

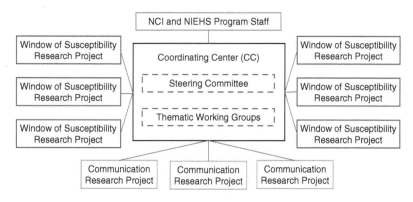

Figure 1.1 Organizational chart of the Breast Cancer and the Environment Research Program

in and of itself, the BCERP aims to give voice to a population that might otherwise be unheard in the research context.

BCERP researchers have examined specific chemicals found in the environment – like bisphenol-A (BPA) and perfluorooctanoic acid (PFOA), among others – and their role as endocrine disruptors that might increase risk of breast cancer later in life. The consequences of different diets, such as those high in animal fats, have also been examined by BCERP biologists using animal models. Additionally, BCERP epidemiologists have followed cohorts of young adolescent girls with regular tracking of urine and blood samples to determine exposure levels and pubertal development. One particular focus of this research is the role of these exposures during puberty, which is a window of susceptibility, or a period of development when mammary glands are undergoing growth or change and are thus more prone to disruption from risk exposures. The triangulation of both human and animal data about environmental exposures, collected by the biology and epidemiology cores, is a key goal of the research program to better understand mechanisms of breast cancer. The COD core, comprised of environmental and breast cancer advocates as well as researchers, also plays an integral role in the BCERP.

BCERP advocates were initially responsible for lobbying of Congress to obtain funding for breast cancer and environment research; they were the catalyst for an initial $35 million dedicated to the first round of seven-year funding for different centers across the United States. From the BCERP's inception, the COD has helped to ensure high retention rates in the epidemiology studies, created and populated websites with BCERP-related educational materials, engaged communities via town hall meetings and educational materials, served on BCERP working groups, engaged in communication research with BCERP partners, and, overall, have maintained an important community/stakeholder presence who provide insights for BCERP scientists. The COD has also initiated communication research activities to better understand their respective and collective audiences so they can develop and tailor appropriate BCERP communication materials about environmental exposures and breast cancer risk reduction recommendations. At the time of this writing, the COD has trained advocates on semi-structured focus group interview techniques to recruit members of their communities to discuss and better understand perceptions of environmental risks of breast cancer as they pertain to the research of the respective biology and epidemiology core members (Silk et al., 2017). This allows for even more fine-grained targeting of the beliefs and values of the unique populations embedded in the advocates' communities who are concerned with the health and well-being of their daughters and of the public at large.

Case 2: financial incentives in normative systems

The second community-engaged, transdisciplinary case, FINS, is a six-year program of research using combined emic-etic studies (i.e., studying phenomena from both within and outside of a group, respectively) of a unique population group designed to identify key lessons from research for the design and implementation of payment for ecosystem-services policies (PES) programs. Most recently funded by the US National Science Foundation's (NSF) Interdisciplinary Behavioral and Social Sciences mechanism (IBSS), this program of work began with a series of internal seed grants to a small team of scientists and support through the United States Department of Agriculture's Hatch Mechanism. PES programs are economic interventions designed to offset the financial costs of conservation behaviors by paying people to conserve, protect, or enhance natural resources. The FINS program currently includes a team of people from a conservation organization, including community researchers (ethnically Tibetan interviewers, surveyors, and experimenters), two universities, and four disciplines (see Figure 1.2). Its ultimate goal is to move a program of research and theory-building on social norms and financial incentives into policy recommendations for the ways in which PES policies are implemented.

Framed in theories of social norms and culture, this FINS research (c.f. Lapinski, Kerr, Zhao, & Shupp, 2017) is being conducted in the Sanjiangyuan area, located in southern Qinghai Province on the Tibetan Plateau (see Figure 1.3), home to about 960,000 inhabitants of whom 90% are ethnically Tibetan and about 70% are pastoralists. The area is ecologically significant because its glaciers and high-altitude grasslands provide significant inputs to three of Asia's major rivers (the Yellow, Yangtze, and Mekong) that provide fresh water downstream to nearly a quarter of the world's population. The grasslands of the Plateau have supported Tibetan nomadic populations for thousands of years and nurtured a unique culture of which a fundamental element is Tibetan Buddhism. Economically dependent mainly on yaks and seasonally available caterpillar fungus, Tibetan society and culture have developed strong self-disciplinary norms about ecological conservation. As such, the Tibetan pastoralists represent a unique population group in that they can be juxtaposed with the dominant ethnically Han culture, and there is evidence for a shared set of values, beliefs, and practices of this group (see work by Yeh, 2012; Yeh & Gaerrang, 2011). Community perspectives have been and continue to be infused throughout the FINS program. For example, decisions about research foci (e.g., herding practices, patrolling for poaching of wild-animals, and to a lesser extent human-bear interactions) were driven by community needs and existing practices and values; design and implementation of the study protocols and instruments

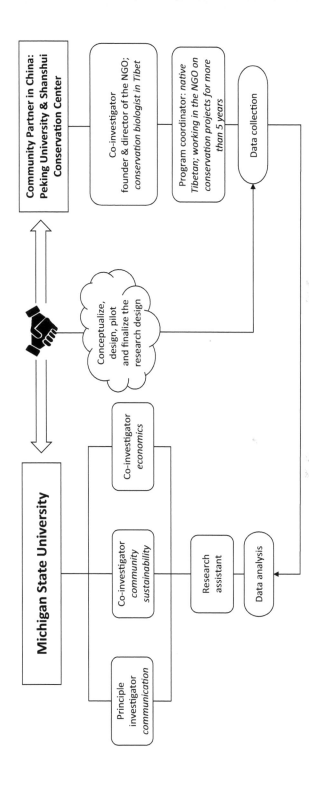

Figure 1.2 An illustration of the collaboration between the US-based research team at Michigan State University and the community partner in China in the FINS project

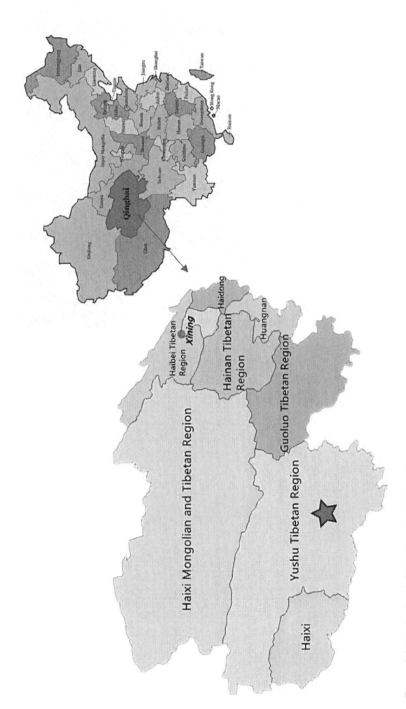

Figure 1.3 Study site in China for the FINS project

Source: Creative Commons – Open Source

were informed through community member input; and, data from the community informed the design of the measures, theoretical model, analysis procedures, and focus of program efforts. Currently, the team is working to design policy recommendations and developing best practices.

Shanshui Conservation Organization, a conservation non-governmental organization (NGO) and collaborator in this program, operates a community-based conservation program using non-cash incentives while also drawing on local norms in favor of conservation. This NGO is engaged with local government officials responsible for conservation and has brokered agreements in which the government has given local people greater responsibility for conservation, including PES programs that pay people to modify their herding practices to protect grassland quality and quantity. The Sanjiangyuan region is a key site for this kind of research because of the existing social structures documented in prior research (e.g., Yeh, 2012), the types of behaviors important for conservation, the research available on the complex cultural dynamics of the region, and the potential to provide input on forthcoming large-scale PES work in the region.

Most PES projects are government- or donor-funded, with budgets subject to political processes and availability of funds. This makes them susceptible to elimination, raising the question of what will happen to the targeted ecosystem-related behaviors after a program ends. The economic models that drive the design of PES programs are ill-equipped to address this question. However, communication science explains the effects of social norms and other psycho-social factors on behaviors, though it has not incorporated the effects of monetary payments (c.f., Lapinski et al., 2017). Substantively, the FINS program looks at the effects of short-term monetary incentives on normative systems and on longer-term behavior. It integrates economic models and models of social norms to explain and predict the ways in which monetary incentives influence social norms and behaviors.

The project outcomes and activities focus on several issues. From a substantive standpoint, the outcomes of the project are two-fold: (1) to design and test culturally derived measures of social norms and the factors associated with normative influence and (2) to design and test a model of PES programs that accounts for the effects of social norms and conservation-related values in economic systems. These outcomes were accomplished through a series of activities, including meetings with cultural insiders, deep discussions among team members about the conceptual foundations of the project ideas, in-depth interviews with community members, a survey of households, and some small field experiments. From an implementation, broader impacts, or translational perspective, the major objective of the FINS program was to determine the meaning of the study findings for the ways in which PES policies and programs are implemented, identify best practices, and disseminate this information to groups that might use it. This activity was accomplished by creating summative documents of all study findings, holding a series of team meetings and discussions with program staff charged with program implementation, and drafting recommendations for practice. These documents were designed to be shared with local conservation organizations and possibly governmental officials in the study region, as well as to NGOs working in China and on PES globally (e.g., Conservation International). This last activity was in-process at the time of this writing. The research and outreach work of the team will ultimately contribute recommendations for implementation of PES programs that avoid crowding out non-monetary motivations for conservation behavior.

Key areas of similarity and difference

In an effort to distill key lessons learned from the BCERP and PES, a number of criteria have been identified to consider for comparison. These criteria represent both macro and micro considerations as individuals move forward with partnerships for environmental communication research. Table 1.1 provides a snapshot of the criteria and a side-by-side comparison with lessons learned. The following section elaborates on a range of criteria to consider as large-scale environmental communication projects are designed and implemented.

Scope and partners

Identification of project scope and the organizations and individuals to be involved represents a key decision as a program or project moves forward. Limiting the scope of a project and clarifying the role of partners in meeting the scope of work needs to be delineated early in the design of project, but there also needs to be some flexibility as projects evolve. The defined scope of the BCERP is to examine environmental factors and their relationship to breast cancer risk, with a focus on windows of susceptibility. The particular scope of these factors includes, as mentioned previously, chemical exposures in common commercial items like BPA, PFOA, and oxybenzone. However, diet has also been included as a factor in one's environment, such that diets high in animal fats have been found to be associated with breast cancer in later life, especially when those diets are had during a window of susceptibility like puberty. Partners have been domestic, but representative of a wide geographic area from the West Coast, Midwest, Northeast, and Southeast parts of the United States. Primary partners have been biologists, epidemiologists, communication scientists, and advocates from both environmental and breast cancer groups. Within the transdisciplinary

Table 1.1 Comparison of environmental communication programs

Criteria	BCERP	FINS	Lesson learned
Scope	Broad	Narrow	Identifying and maintaining a scope that is reasonable given the partners and resources available.
Partners	Domestic	International	Regardless of geography, a clear understanding of partnership parameters and roles is necessary.
Level of community participation	High	Moderate	For community partnerships to work, community groups need to be full partners at all levels of the research/project.
Complexity of structure	High	Low	Partnering with different stakeholders is complex due to varying cultures, goals, and priorities that need to be valued.
Relationship building/trust	High	High	This takes time and requires long-term commitment beyond grant cycles.
Capacity building	Moderate	Moderate	Ultimately, models need to support the long-term needs of community partners and help build capacity.
Decision-making	Shared	Shared	Partnerships require shared decision-making about project. Setting up processes is essential.
Transdisciplinarity	High	High	These are problems that are bigger than one discipline and require different stakeholders around the table.
Time	Extensive	Extensive	Time to complete work is elongated due to the need to honor stakeholder input and relationships.
Community partner budget	Inadequate	Extensive	Community partners need to be budgeted into projects fairly to support their time and efforts; they are not simply volunteers.
Audiences	Parents, young girls, advocates, pediatric HCPs	Tibetan pastoralists, policy-makers	Priority audiences must be identified. Extending beyond them to increase reach of environmental communication to other groups is a long-term endeavor.
Organization	Coordinating center model, working groups, steering committee	Team model, independent working groups	Organizational structures can be specified in advance of project implementation and modified throughout the course of the program as necessary.

model, there is an expectation that opportunities to partner in novel ways will evolve as the partners collaborate, which allows for innovative science that may span the boundaries of the original scope of work.

The FINS program started as a collaboration among academics from various disciplines and then expanded to the current project team with the inclusion of a community partner (i.e., Shanshui Conservation Center; see Figure 1.2). It has had a fixed set of partners for the life of the current funding cycle, but is expanding as the team begins to look more closely at the ecological changes connected to social changes. Although the overarching focus of the project (i.e., the long-term effects of short-term financial incentives on social norms) has changed very little and the team's focus on PES programs and policies remains constant, the context and details of the scope of work continue to evolve with new findings. That is, as our data and discussions with project partners indicate particular areas of inquiry and application are more or less fruitful and relevant, the project activities have shifted accordingly. Importantly, for both programs, the deliverables promised to funders have allowed for this to occur, but this kind of flexibility is something not all funding mechanisms/funders will abide.

Level of community participation

When it is appropriate to forge partnerships between researchers and community groups, identifying the nature of that collaboration and the level at which it is useful for all collaborators is key. The BCERP attempts to involve community partners across all areas of the project. Working groups, requests for proposals for opportunity funds, publication guidelines, representation on the program's steering committee, and all other facets of the project strive to ensure that the voices of community partners are heard and provide insight at all levels of the project. This approach creates an equitable structure where community partners' input is not only heard, but valued.

In the case of the FINS project, early iterations began by talking with community organizations globally (in particular, Conservation International) about the relevance of some of the team's ideas for the work they do, as well as places they saw gaps in their understanding of people's response to their PES activities. This involved in-depth discussions with Conservation International field and program staff as well as a field visit to a PES reforestation project. For the portion of our work that is funded by the NSF, Shanshui Conservation Organization served as an equal partner in the project design and implementation, including having a named co-investigator on the award. The project deliverables and budget included specific activities to bring community voices to the table and ultimately to take the program findings to policy-makers and other stakeholders.

Complexity of structure

When addressing large, real-world problems with community-engaged approaches, complexity in structure and implementation is certain. The BCERP is a large group of stakeholders with an expansive goal to investigate the role of environmental factors in breast cancer. There are many regions, scientists from different disciplines, community partners, a coordinating center with many resources to assist the program's implementation, a steering committee, government agency representatives, multiple core groups (EPI, BIO, and COD), working groups, and each individual site has its own structure with associated meetings (e.g., the MSU team has three separate monthly meetings for respective groups). There are also individual committees that evolve for planning the annual integration and annual meeting for the BCERP.

For any given member of the BCERP, it is a substantial time commitment to participate in meetings, particularly for those with greater involvement. Within this structure are competing goals of different stakeholders that need to be understood and valued. For example, while all stakeholders have buy-in and support the overarching aim of investigating environmental risk factors, they each have other goals to keep their community advocacy groups satisfied, informed, and funded so they are meeting their individual advocacy missions. Valuing these different primary and secondary goals for participating in the BCERP will facilitate meeting goals and partner needs.

The FINS is a smaller project with a simple partnership model between a group of researchers from different disciplines and a non-governmental, community-based, environmental organization. The most complex aspects of the structure involve the research implementation model which has involved a network of translators, data collection staff, field supervisors, and researchers to allow for data collection to occur. Team members from the conservation organization coordinate the connections with local policymakers and government officials which helped guide the project development to a small extent and will be crucial as the project findings are disseminated.

Relationship building and trust

All strong partnerships develop from a position of mutual trust, but this does indeed take time to develop. Understanding the need for partnerships to develop, the BCERP, originally the Breast Cancer and the Environment Research Center (BCERC), was funded for seven years in its first round. Such a period of funding is uncommon, but the pioneering nature of the project necessitated a longer commitment early in the project to help facilitate the partnerships and science that would evolve from those partnerships. Trust cannot be manufactured, and trust takes time when there are a range of specific aims and objectives to be met for the project, competing goals across different stakeholders, and the integration of different project components in an often highly emotionally charged advocate environment.

As for the FINS, the initial project team formed organically and took advantage of a small amount of internal university funds to seed the project. The NSF project funds, which span four years, was a result of two years of working together, field work, and building relationships with potential partners and community groups. Trust among project partners has been built largely through consistent contact among team members: the local team meets weekly and the larger team meets regularly using virtual meetings, in additional to in-person meetings that happen in the field at least annually. This is something that has been negotiated through the life of the project. There were several times where team members in China expressed their dissatisfaction with their connection to project activities and as a result, the project team implemented changes to procedures to provide greater opportunities to connect. Busy schedules, working across time zones, and language differences add complexity to the project.

Homophily of team members helped to build trust initially. For example, the lead from the conservation organization is a conservation biology researcher and the organization has a research-driven model of decision-making. Because of this, the team shared perspectives on the value of both social and natural science research. A second factor that has impacted trust is the completion of project deliverables by team members. The project activities have progressed consistently through the life of the project largely by using regular team meetings and retreats as a mechanism for team members holding themselves and each other accountable to the project.

Capacity building

Capacity building is not always salient for project stakeholders, but is critical for the longevity of projects. Capacity building is the idea that program efforts should help to inform how the community can do what they do with greater ease, efficiency, reach, or effectiveness. Perhaps this is through new processes, people, or resources – regardless, the capacity building ideas need to evolve from a partnered perspective. In the case of the BCERP, program activities can provide advocates and community partners with resources, networks, and funds to meet their individual missions that align with BCERP goals. The use of funds and resources, ultimately in service of the BCERP, provides additional benefit to the individual partner organizations' sustainability.

In the case of FINS, a stated goal of the project team was building the capacity of the staff of the conservation organization in terms of social science methods, data collection, analysis, and reporting. These needs and the ability of the project to meet these needs continue to evolve as the project moves forward. The second aspect of capacity building is using data from the project to inform the community implementation of PES. This is just the beginning as the team synthesizes and integrates the project findings.

Decision-making processes

In collaborative projects, there need to be clear processes for how decisions will be made. In other words, there should be a clear document for what decision-making modality will be invoked when large project decisions are to be made. For example, will a working group make the decision in the BCERP, an individual principal investigator (PI), or the BCERP Coordinating Center? Will the decision be an individual mandate (PI), consensus decision (100% agreement), majority rules (a vote where a quorum is necessary and 51% vote carries), or a small powerful minority (steering committee decision)? Further, in what circumstances will it be necessary to invoke decision-making processes? These processes are typically ignored in research collaborations and thus there is a lack of clarity that leads to groups feeling disenfranchised and "not heard" as equal partners in the project. In part because of the small scope of the FINS, no decision-making model was specified for the team, and decisions have been made largely by consensus or fiat depending on an issue's urgency.

Transdisciplinarity

Environmental challenges will not be solved by one discipline, as they are multifaceted and complicated; thus, the use of transdisciplinary models is necessary. For the BCERP and the FINS program, a transdisciplinary scope has been essential. For the BCERP, a question that has been posed is whether or not it would have accomplished more or less if it did not have a transdisciplinary focus. There is not a straightforward answer to this question, but there is clear evidence that the ongoing interaction between the disciplines has led to novel questions and an increased ability to more nimbly move in those novel directions. For example, the triangulation of data from animal and human studies has had heuristic value that may have taken much longer had scientists not partnered with the BCERP. And because the BCERP adopts the precautionary principle, in which precautionary measures are taken against some potentially (albeit not entirely verified) risk to human and/or environmental health, advocates have more quickly shared risk reduction messages with lay audiences than perhaps they would have by using a different research model.

The transdisciplinary scope of the FINS program was fundamental to all aspects of the team's work. That is to say, the tasks could not be accomplished without the transdisciplinary team. The genesis of the work is an integration of theories from communication and economics; therefore, the methods and approaches cut across these disciplines. The community organizations involved in the project impacted the design of the theoretical models and the context for application of both the ideas and outcomes of the project. Although the complexity of working across disciplines can sometimes reduce the efficiency of task accomplishment, in the case of FINS, it would not exist without each of the program partners.

Application of theory

A challenge for community-based partnerships and transdisciplinary collaborations is to maintain a rigorous application of communication and behavior change theory throughout all aspects of programming. The BCERP is unified around the central theme of understanding the environmental link to breast cancer and disseminating those findings for risk reduction activities. Across the collaboration, there are diverse ways of knowing and methods of inquiry that are employed. On one hand, this is an advantage as it challenges partners to be clear on exactly what their research and activities mean in the greater scope of the project. In addition, it allows for unique understandings of the problem of breast cancer. On the other hand, it can be difficult at times to fully communicate, say, the benefit of one theoretical framework over another or the usefulness of a particular social scientific method to biology and epidemiology partners. This lack of theoretical and methodological unity can impede intra-organization understanding, but can also push partners in all cores to be realistic about how substantive their work is and inspire more innovative strategies. It also allows for more flexibility in planning program activities, as theories and methods can be seen as elements in a toolbox, in which one may be best suited to address a particular part of a problem.

As for the FINS, theoretical concepts were integrated from communication sciences and economics into a single economic model to explain the long-term impacts of short-term incentives on social norms and behavior. Whereas a typical economic model characterizes the effects of conservation payments as promoting conservation behavior and thus improving ecosystem conditions, according to this integrated model, the conservation payments and the resulting actions both influence social norms and in turn are influenced by social norms. Feedback from changes in ecosystem conditions also influences actions. Throughout the course of the entire project, each stage of the research has been carefully designed and implemented to stick to this overarching framework. In addition to regular in-person and virtual meetings between the team at MSU and Shanshui, throughout the life of the project, team members traveled between the two organizations on a regular basis for long working sessions. For example, a week-long intensive workshop was held in July 2016. Two researchers from the MSU team traveled to Xining, China, where Shanshui's main office is located, and convened collaborators to discuss the scope, theory-building, and progress of the project.

Time

Community-based partnerships take time not only to develop but also to implement. The more individuals who join a team, the more time it will take to understand their concerns, gather their input, and engage with them as substantive team members. In the BCERP, every COD-related project has taken longer than projected. Although this is true most of the time in research, it is particularly true with community-based models. There are basic challenges of how to get everyone on regular conference calls, resolve research ethics issues (e.g. IRB requirements) that accompany multi-site projects, and understand that many community partners are volunteers and even breast cancer survivors managing serious health issues. Similar challenges have faced the FINS team: time-zone barriers; long trips to study sites; and moving across English, Mandarin, and Tibetan have increased the time required to complete project activities despite full commitment and engagement on the part of all project team members.

Audiences/population

Translational efforts for the BCERP have focused on a number of audiences, particularly mothers of young girls who can influence their daughters' behavior during a window of susceptibility to environmental cancer risk factors. Translating emerging science into usable messages for lay audiences requires cooperation from scientists, as they are not always ready to share risk reduction messages from their research, and certainly not before their findings are published.

A central feature of the FINS program is the characteristics of the unique population on which it is focused. The grassland ecosystem on the Plateau has supported Tibetan pastoralists, who have historically been nomadic, for thousands of years, and nurtured a unique culture of which Tibetan Buddhism is a key element; including a strong norm for individual behaviors that encourage people to live in harmony with, and respect, the land, water and all living beings (Shen & Tan, 2012). Tibetans living in the Shanshui region have made significant contributions to conservation and are, perhaps, the primary reason why large numbers of wildlife still roam freely on the Plateau. Translation of findings in this project is designed to happen at two levels: (1) for partner staff and leadership, which include members of the ethnic Tibetan population and (2) for policy-makers and conservation leaders who implement PES policies. The first has occurred throughout the life of the project and corresponds to capacity building. The second is just beginning as a final phase in the funded activities, which will be led by the conservation team members.

Community partner role and budget

The idea of community partners needing a budget to do their required work for the grant project is counterintuitive for some scientists. One perspective is that community partners are volunteers and they are doing the work as part of their volunteer endeavors – so, why would time be budgeted for those efforts? Ultimately, this perspective is problematic as some granting agencies are now requiring a high level of partnership for translational purposes. Similarly, in the case of federal or state funders, citizens whose taxes may pay for research have an inherent right to be informed in a useable way about the emerging science their taxes are paying for. This may seem simplistic, but it takes expertise, networks, and time. Community partners can provide this expertise, networks, and time, but it is at a cost to them and they should receive appropriate compensation for their efforts. For the FINS project, the community partnering organization was part of the design of all project activities including the budget; capacity for budget management was high at all institutions although administration varied.

Some BCERP sites have funded their community partners very well and some have provided less of a budget for activities. This is an area where community partners may need training so they can negotiate appropriately at the start of a grant submission for the necessary resources required for the work requested. It is also a case where capacity building can occur for all project partners at all levels of a program of work. For example, MSU has a community outreach and engagement certificate program designed to train current and future researchers on aspects of community-based projects. Like universities and research institutions, community organizations vary in their ability to manage budgets. Again, this area is ripe for capacity building activities and coordination early in project activities.

Concluding thoughts

This chapter provided an overview and analysis of two very different programs of environmental communication research and engagement with unique populations. Our purpose here was to identify key dimensions of the programs, critically and reflectively examine them, and ultimately describe the promise and pitfalls of these programs in order to facilitate other efforts in this space. These two programs, which span over 20 years total, provide different models for stakeholder engagement, interdisciplinary collaboration, and moving environmental communication research into practice. They use different models for understanding and connecting with domestic and international unique population groups. This chapter has addressed the challenges of complex projects, including incorporation of diverse viewpoints, reconciling conflicting goals, and building capacity to work together. If health communication offers an example, environmental communication scholars should continue their efforts to work closely with groups and people who put research into practice. The community-driven, participatory models of environmental communication facilitate valuable connections among groups who need each other to solve, or at least address, complex problems. Not to be overly dramatic, but the future of the planet may depend on it.

Acknowledgement

Partial support was provided by the USDA National Institute of Food and Agriculture, Hatch project numbers MICL02244 and MICL02296, by National Science Foundation Award #SMA-1328503, and NIEHS Award Numbers U01 ES026119 and R21 ES027418.

References

The Ad Council. (2017). *Smokey's history*. Retrieved from https://smokeybear.com/en/smokeys-history/about-the-campaign

Centers for Disease Control and Prevention. (2017). *Effective interventions*. Retrieved March 18, 2018 from https://effectiveinterventions.cdc.gov/

Falk-Krzesinski, H. J., Contractor, N., Fiore, S. M., Hall, K. L., Kane, C., Keyton, J., . . . & Trochim, W. (2011). Mapping a research agenda for the science of team science. *Research Evaluation, 20*, 145–158. doi:10.3152/095820211X12941371876580

Harvard School of Public Health. (2012). *Harvard transdisciplinary research center in energetic and cancer center*. Retrieved from www.hsph.harvard.edu/trec/about-us/definitions/

Kreps, G. L., & Maibach, E. W. (2008). Transdisciplinary science: The nexus between communication and public health. *Journal of Communication, 58*, 732–748. doi:10.1111/j.1460-2466.2008.00411.x

Lapinski, M. K., Kerr, J. M., Zhao, J., & Shupp, R. S. (2017). Social norms, behavioral payment programs, and cooperative behaviors: Toward a theory of financial incentives in normative systems. *Human Communication Research, 43*, 148–171. doi:10.1111/hcre.12099

Lapinski, M. K., Randall, L. M., Peterson, M., Peterson, A., & Klein, K. A. (2009). Prevention options for positives: The effects of a health communication intervention for men who have sex with men living with HIV/AIDS. *Health Communication, 24*, 562–571. doi:10.1080/10410230903104947

Mitchell, P. H. (2005). What's in a name? Multidisciplinary, interdisciplinary, and transdisciplinary. *Journal of Professional Nursing, 21*, 332–334. doi:10.1016/j.profnurs.2005.10.009

Neuhauser, L., Kreps, G. L., & Syme, S. L. (2014). Community participatory design of health communication interventions. In D. K. Kim, A. Singhal, & G. L. Kreps (Eds.), *Health communication: Strategies for developing global health programs* (pp. 227–243). New York, NY: Peter Lang.

Neuberger, L., Silk, K. J., Yun, D., Bowman, N. D., & Anderson, J. (2011). Concern as a motivation for protection: An investigation of mothers' concern about daughters' breast cancer risk. *Journal of Health Communication, 16*, 1055–1071. doi:10.1080/10810730.2011.571339

Oetzel, J., Simpson, M., Berryman, K., Iti, T., & Reddy, R. (2015). Managing communication tensions and challenges during the end-of-life journey: Perspectives of Māori kaumātua and their whānau. *Health Communication, 30*, 350–360. doi:10.1080/10410236.2013.861306

Orbe, M. P. (1998). *Constructing co-cultural theory: An explication of culture, power, and communication.* Thousand Oaks, CA: SAGE.

O'Rourke, M., & Crowley, S. (2013). Philosophical intervention and cross-disciplinary science: The story of the Toolbox Project. *Synthese, 190*, 1937–1954. doi:10.1007/s11229-012-0175-y

Rice, R. E., & Atkin, C. K. (2012). *Public communication campaigns.* Newbury Park, CA: SAGE.

Shen, X., & Tan, J. (2012). Ecological conservation, cultural preservation, and a bridge between: The journey of Shanshui Conservation Center in the Sanjiangyuan Region, Qinghai-Tibetan Plateau, China. *Ecology and Society, 17*. doi:10.5751/ES-05345-170438

Silk, K. J., & Smith, S. W. (2016). Organizing transdisciplinary research: A breast cancer and the environment collaborative model. In T. R. Harrison & E. A. Williams (Eds.), *Organizations, communication, and health* (pp. 297–312). New York, NY: Routledge.

Silk, K. J., Totzkay, D., Rakoff, M., Serrano, M., Burke, K., Miller, K., . . . & Symington, A. (2017). Preliminary results of the COD opportunity fund project: Understanding audiences. Presented at the *12th Annual Meeting of the Breast Cancer and the Environment Research Program*, Monrovia, CA.

Stokols, D. (2006). Toward a science of transdisciplinary action research. *American Journal of Community Psychology, 38,* 63–77. doi:10.1007/s10464-006-9060-5

Yeh, E. T. (2012). Transnational environmentalism and entanglements of sovereignty: The tiger campaign across the Himalayas. *Political Geography, 31,* 408–418. doi:10.1016/j.polgeo.2012.06.003

Yeh, E. T., & Gaerrang. (2011). Tibetan pastoralism in neoliberalising China: Continuity and change in Gouli. *Area, 43,* 165–172. doi:10.1111/j.1475-4762.2010.00976.x

2 The vanishing racial divide

The dynamics of race and socioeconomic class in environmental risk communication

B.F. Battistoli

Introduction

Although there is some disagreement in the scientific community about the starting point and probable duration of the period of climate-driven disasters we are experiencing as a result of global warming, there is general agreement that they are unprecedented in the historically brief reign of Homo sapiens as the dominant species on the planet. As we struggle to come to grips with these phenomena, the need for development of effective risk communication methods has never been greater.

Risk communication is an emerging discipline, with a history that extends little more than 30 years (Leiss & Powell, 1997). The efforts of risk communication researchers and practitioners cannot be separated from the social and cultural environment in which they occur. In the United States, one of the primary challenges to the efforts to deal with the deleterious effects of climate change is the struggle to understand the relationship between race and socioeconomic class. As Fothergill, Maestas, and Darlington (1999) noted:

> It is true that racial and ethnic communities are disproportionately poor in the US, and that the proportion of poor among racial and ethnic minorities are growing. Yet, it is important that we do not dismiss issues of race and ethnicity. While in many ways they cannot be separated from issues of economic resources and power, in other ways they explain marginalization in the disaster experience in a manner that socioeconomic factors cannot.
>
> (p. 169)

Nearly two decades after Fothergill et al.'s study was published, risk communication researchers and practitioners still struggle to reconcile race and socioeconomic class in the risk communication equation, and to integrate that reconciliation into research methodologies, models, and, perhaps most importantly, into the design and implementation of effective risk management message campaigns. To attempt such reconciliation under unprecedented environmental stress is a daunting task.

The impending storm

Humans began reshaping the planet through their dominance over flora and fauna about 50,000 years ago, during the Pleistocene Period (Bello, 2013). The effects of that reshaping increased over centuries to the present day, in which we have become one of the primary influences on the environment. Scientists are not in agreement as to when the tipping point occurred. Some place it 7,000 years ago, with the advent of agriculture. Others place it as recently as the Industrial Age in the late 19th century, when humans began their fateful romance with fossil fuels. Others mark it at 1945, with the advent of the Atomic Age at the end of World War II. Although there is not widespread agreement as to *when* it started, there is general agreement on *what* it started: The Anthropocene Period (ibid). What is unknown, of course, is when, or how, Earth's most recent period will end. But its start has certainly been tempestuous, and climate scientists are working to understand its implications for the future.

The report of the US Global Climate Change Research Program, entitled "Global Climate Change Impacts in the United States" (Karl, Melillo, & Peterson, 2009), offers a comprehensive list of what the authors term "key messages," the likely effects of global climate change on the US, placed within a historical scientific context. Its predictions for the US climate include rising average temperatures, increased precipitation (both in total and per storm event), increase in the frequency and intensity of extreme weather events such as heatwaves and droughts, increased intensity of cyclonic storms, declining arctic ice and rising sea levels.

Karl et al. (2009) note that the average US temperature has increased by more than 2°F over the past 50 years, a trend that is expected to continue. Cutting emissions now will only affect the future, since this rise is driven by emissions that occurred in the past. How high temperatures will reach is a matter of debate, with most predictions occurring in a range of +4°F–+11°F by the end of this century (p. 29). As noted by McMichael, Woodruff, and Hales (2006), increased temperatures can be lethal. Using a model based on "medium-level emissions climate change" to predict climate impact in Australia, they project a 50% annual increase in deaths in its large cities as a direct result of excess heat (p. 864). Such events are already occurring. During the record heatwave that struck Chicago in July 1995 and lasted for 10 days, daytime air temperatures were in excess of 100 degrees, indoor air temperatures exceeded 120 degrees in high-rise apartments, and 521 Chicago residents died "directly from heat-related causes" (Klinenberg, 2002).

Advances in research methods and modeling have enabled scientists to develop detailed descriptions of climate change events throughout the history of the planet. Ely et al. (1992) studied flooding patterns over the past 50 centuries in the area that is now the southwestern United States. Their findings suggest that "transitional climatic periods," such as the one we are presently experiencing, with marked changes in climatic conditions, may produce the "highest hydrologic variance" (p. 410). Reuveny (2007) notes that in the period 1975–2001, some 30,000 people in North America were affected by drought, while some 800,000 were affected by floods (ibid, p. 661). Schwartz and Randall (2003) explored the potential impact of climate change on US national security. They described an "abrupt climate change scenario," in which "Paleoclimatic evidence suggests that altered climatic patterns could last for as much as a century" (ibid, p. 1).

The increased intensity of tropical cyclones is a matter of record, with Hurricanes Harvey and Irma the most recent examples on the US mainland (Battistoli, King, & White, 2017). Elsner and Jagger (2008) used climatic modeling to predict "stronger cyclones in a warming future," though they noted that other models predict a decrease in the frequency of such storms (p. 679). Henderson-Sellers et al. (1998) note the difficulty of predicting the frequency and intensity of cyclonic activity with an acceptable degree of accuracy (p. 24). But Ulbrich, Pinto, Kupfer, Leckebusch, Spangehl, and Reyers (2008) used a computer model that generated a comparison of the periods 1960–2000 and 2081–2100, and found increases in storm activity in both the Pacific and Atlantic oceans in the future (p. 1674).

Rahmstorf (2007) argues that the present period of anthropogenic warming is comparable to the magnitude of warming that occurred in the transition from the pre-industrial to the industrial age. His findings include "a projected sea-level rise in 2100 of 0.5–1.4 meters [1.64–4.59 feet] above the 1990 level" (p. 368). Karl et al. (2009) note that based upon just a two-foot rise in global sea level by 2100, the relative sea-level rise in New York City would be 2.3 feet, 2.9 feet at Hampton Roads, Virginia, and 3.5 feet at Galveston, Texas (p. 37).

McMichael, Woodruff, Whetton, Whetton et al. (2003) note that although regional populations are resilient, developing techniques to adjust to changing climate conditions, extreme events can stress populations beyond the limits of adaptation (p. 860). O'Brien, O'Keefe, Rose, and Wisner (2006) argue that climate change is a "complex and protracted hazard" that negatively affects the resilience of populations seeking to adapt to it (pp. 71–72).

Risking race: the emerging discipline of risk communication struggles to reconcile racial difference

The database that climatic scientists use to explore climatic changes on the planet to aid in their understanding of the climatic transition we are experiencing comprises millions of years. In contrast, the database that social scientists who study risk communication rely upon covers little more than a century. "Risk communication" is in its infancy as a field of academic study. While most scholars trace the origins of modern communication studies to the mass society theories of World War I 100 years ago (Baran & Davis, 2011), Leiss and Powell (1997) noted that the phrase "risk communication" did not appear in the literature until 1984, as noted in the earliest references in Rohrmann, Wiedemann, and Stegelmann (1990).

Leis and Powell (1997) offer a general definition of risk communication and an operational definition of risk. First, the general: "Risk communication is the process of exchanges about how best to assess and manage risks among academics, regulatory practitioners, interest groups, and the general public" (p. 33), and second, the operational: "Risk is the probability of harm in any given situation, and this probability is determined by two factors: (a) the nature of a hazard and (b) the extent of anyone's exposure to that hazard" (p. 33). Morgan, Fischoff, Bostrom, and Atman (2002) offer a definition of risk communication that focuses on its recipients: "Communication intended to supply laypeople with the information they need to make informed, independent judgments about risks to health, safety, and the environment" (p. 4).

In their exploration of risk communication among minority and low-income populations, Rowel, Sheikhattari, Barber, and Evans-Halland (2012) cited the operational definition of "crisis and risk communication" offered by the Centers for Disease Control (2009):

> Crisis and emergency risk communication is the capability to provide accurate, credible, actionable, and timely information to the public in culturally and linguistically appropriate ways to inform decision making and reduce uncertainty before, during, and after a public health emergency. It involves an iterative process of developing, coordinating, and disseminating information to the public, responding to inquiries and reactions from the public, and evaluating the effectiveness of the information provided and the delivery channels utilized.
>
> (CDC, 2009, p. 43)

In an analysis of national survey data on the location of hazardous waste facilities, Flynn, Slovic, and Mertz (1994) acknowledged the difficulty, if not impossibility, of separating race from socioeconomic status. In addition to race, they identified other significant factors in site selection for these facilities including low levels of income and education, economic vulnerability, and political weakness (p. 1104). Bolin and Bolton (1986) found it similarly difficult to separate race from socioeconomic status in their study of housing types, quality, and location in areas subject to natural disaster (ibid, p. 216). Peacock and Girard (1997) argue that, "Race and ethnicity are linked to housing quality – not because of ethnically based cultural variations as is true in some societies – but because race and ethnicity are still important determinants of the economic resources, such as income and credit, critical for obtaining housing" (ibid, p. 173).

Barry (1997) notes the unequal effect of natural disasters on minority communities, citing the Mississippi River flood of 1927, in which local, state and federal officials attempted to spare White communities by dynamiting the levees protecting predominantly Black St. Bernard and Plaquemines parishes, allowing the river to inundate them. By virtue of their financial insecurity, the poor are at risk before a natural disaster strikes, lacking the financial resources to either prepare for disaster or recover from it (Morrow, 1999; National Academy of Sciences, 2006; Fothergill & Peek, 2004). In a study of the deadly Chicago heatwave of 1995, Klinenberg (2002) found that the demographic variables of race, age, and socioeconomic class were all factors in heat-related deaths (ibid, pp. 81–83).

The premise of racial difference is well established in risk communication, but research into the phenomenon has come a long way from its beginnings in the late 20th century. In 1986, Bolin and Bolton included Blacks among the demographic groups that seemed to be "less vulnerable" to the "stresses of disaster" (Bolin & Bolton, 1986, p. 14). In 1999, Fothergill et al. argued that the links between socioeconomic status, ethnicity, and race in risk communication deserved further exploration (Fothergill et al., 1999). In 2012, Rowel et al. noted "the disproportional impact of disasters among low-income minority populations" (Rowel et al., 2012, p. 125).

Bates, Fogleman, Parenton, Pittman, and Tracy (1963) noted that although the number of Whites and Blacks who lost their lives when Hurricane Audrey struck Cameron Parish, Louisiana on July 27, 1957, was relatively equal (215 Whites, 190 Blacks), the percentages of each population lost were not – 3.80% of Whites lost their lives, while 32.59% of Black residents perished (ibid, p. 127). They offered three hypotheses to explain the disparity, in language representative of the prevailing attitudes on race at that time, which include insights into socioeconomic factors, and a fourth that is jarring when viewed through current perspectives on race:

> There were a number of reasons for the differential loss. First, the Negro Front Ridge community was located on the lowest ridge in the area, and

was situated closer to the Gulf than other communities. Because of this, it suffered greater and more prolonged impact, especially from the rising waters. Secondly, it appears that virtually no evacuation took place from the Negro community. This is possibly accounted for by the availability of fewer automobiles and of money to finance evacuation. A third possible reason lies in the fact that Negro housing was not as substantial as that in the white community. Only four out of 70 houses were left on Front Ridge after the storm, while many more houses in the other areas survived with relatively minor damage. It is also possible that the Negroes in this area, being generally less well educated, were less prone to listen to warnings than were the whites. But this can't be proved.

(p. 128)

When Hurricane Andrew made landfall in Miami in the early hours of Monday morning, August 24, 1992, local residents had received only three days warning of the impending storm, as earlier predictions had it breaking up over the Atlantic prior to making landfall (Peacock, Morrow, & Gladwin, 1997, p. 2). Instead, it was a Category 4+ hurricane that cut an 18-mile-wide swath through Southern Dade County (ibid, p. 3). People of color were the majority of the population in the area hit, with Hispanics making up 49.2% and Blacks 20.6%. Gladwin and Peacock (1997) surveyed the population three months after the hurricane and found a consensus that, "ethnic minorities are less likely to evacuate than Anglos" (ibid, p. 66). They argue that economic status had more influence on decisions to evacuate than did race or ethnicity. They found that, "People with higher incomes are more able to and, thus, more likely to evacuate," and "People living in small households are more likely to be mobile and able to evacuate" (ibid, p. 66).

Spence, Lachlan, and Griffin (2007) studied racial differences in accessing risk communication information in the New Orleans area prior to Hurricane Katrina, which struck the Gulf Coast of Louisiana and Mississippi on August 29, 2005. When it came to accessing risk messages from television, they found no significant difference based upon race. In a study of trust in sources of risk communication messages in post-Katrina New Orleans, Battistoli (2016) found that socioeconomic status and frequency of exposure to messages each had a significant positive correlation to trust, while race did not. Elliott and Pais (2006) found that household income, not race, was the best predictor of who evacuated and who remained in their homes as Hurricane Katrina approached (p. 308). They caution that, "race and class, while analytically distinct, constitute overlapping systems of social stratification that remain experientially entangled and causally circular" (p. 298).

Discussion

In a paper entitled, "The social amplification of risk: A conceptual framework," which has become one of the cornerstones in modern risk communication research, Kasperson et al. (1988) argue for the development of a theory that incorporates all the elements and parameters identified to date: "A comprehensive theory is needed that is capable of integrating the technical analysis of risk and the cultural, social, and individual response structures that shape the public experience" (p. 178). To date, the design of such an integrative theory has eluded the discipline of risk communication, despite efforts that extend back more than a decade.

The idea of racial difference has been ingrained in the American culture since pre-colonial times. We tend to think of slavery in terms of the nascent republic, when it was a major point (if not *the* major point) of contention between the northern (primarily non-slaveholder) and the southern (primarily slaveholder) colonies in the negotiation of the Constitution, through the Civil War, Reconstruction, the Jim Crow era, the Civil Right struggles, and beyond. But the roots of slavery in North America extend far beyond the meetings of the Continental Congress in Philadelphia in 1776 that marked the beginning of the republic. America is about to "celebrate" an ignominious milestone, the quadricentennial of the arrival of the first Black slaves at Jamestown in 1619 (HISTORY.com).

Although it would be naïve to expect that a concept of racial difference inculcated in American culture for more than 400 years can be overcome by a discipline little more than three decades old, it is incumbent on risk communication researchers and practitioners to attempt to do so, because the stakes are so high. The environmental challenges facing us are unprecedented, and it is critical that we develop effective risk communication theory and practices to lessen the loss of life they are likely to bring. This review of the literature suggests some ways forward.

First, demography. Any potential solutions must be data-driven, and all demographic variables should receive full consideration in the construction of statistical models of risk communication. Although the studies reviewed here found varying relationships between race and socioeconomic class in the risk communication process, many reveal the existence of a dynamic relationship between and among the variables that express those qualities. Glick (2007) found a significant relationship between the "sociodemographic characteristics" of risk message recipients and their ability to receive, process, and act on warning messages. Fothergill et al. (1999) argue that successful risk communication strategies start with identification and understanding of the diversity issues unique to the target area, and that strategic planning efforts contain measures to ensure that the "disaster reduction process" is inclusive (p. 168).

Second, geography. Risk communication is site-specific. The environmental challenges are unique to the geography, topography, and climate of the site, and the risk communication process that occurs within it cannot be separated from the social and cultural environment in which it occurs. From a mathematical perspective, Renn and Klinke (2012) argue that any statistical analysis of risk must first consider the spatial and temporal factors of the risk environment.

Third, adaptability. It is imperative that we develop statistically reliable risk communication strategies that can be rapidly and effectively deployed in the face of environmental challenges in disparate sites with unique population demographics. Reynolds and Seeger (2005) note that, "efforts have been made to combine notions of risk communication and crisis communication into a practice described as crisis and emergency risk communication," and that the products of those efforts "must be strategic, broad based, responsive, and highly contingent" (p. 49).

The concept of a racial divide is part of the cultural fabric, and its influence has affected many areas of society, including communication research. This phenomenon has affected the design, implementation, and analysis of risk management campaigns. Essentially, it has created an additional step on the "front end" and "back end" of the risk messaging process. Fortunately, studies that treat race and ethnicity in the same manner as other demographic variables continue to be added to the literature, bringing a welcome openness to the data and resultant findings (Gladwin & Peacock, 1997; Fothergill et al., 1999; Fothergill & Peek, 2004; Elliott & Pais, 2006; Battistoli, 2016). It is incumbent upon us to continue to build upon this increased understanding, using the tools at our command to create theories, models, and risk communication campaigns to meet the unprecedented environmental challenges we face.

References

Baran, S. J., & Davis, D. K. (2011). *Mass communication theory: Foundations, ferment, and future*. Canada: Nelson Education.

Barry, J. M. (1997). *Rising tide: The Great Mississippi Flood of 1927 and how it changed America*. New York, NY: Simon & Schuster.

Bates, F. L., Fogleman, C. W., Parenton, V. J., Pittman, R. H., & Tracy, G. S. (1963). *The social and psychological consequences of a natural disaster: A longitudinal study of hurricane Audrey*. Washington, DC: National Academy of Sciences – National Research Council (Publication 1081).

Battistoli, B. F. (2016). Evaluating elements of trust: Race and class in risk communication in post-Katrina New Orleans. *Public Understanding of Science*, *25*(4), 480–489.

Battistoli, B. F., King, T., & White, E. (2017, December). Voices in the storm: The lost discourse of climate change in Hurricanes Harvey and Irma. *International Journal of Crisis Communication, 1,* 72–78.

Bello, D. (2013, December 6). How long have humans dominated the planet. *Scientific American.* Retrieved from www.scientificamerican.com/article/length-of-human-domination/

Bolin, R. C., & Bolton, P. A. (1986). *Race, religion, and ethnicity in disaster recovery.* FMHI Publications Paper No. 88. Retrieved from http://scholarcommons.usf.edu/fmhi_pub/88

Centers for Disease Control and Prevention. (2009). Public health emergency preparedness cooperative agreements budget period 10 performance measures guidance (August 10, 2009 to August 9, 2010). Outcome Monitoring and Evaluation Branch. Retrieved from http://www.bt.cdc.gov/cdcpreparedness/coopagreement/10/FINAL_BP10_PHEP_Performance_Measures_Guidance_May_2010.pdf

Elliott, J. R., & Pais, J. (2006). Race, class, and hurricane Katrina: Social differences in human responses to disaster. *Social Science Research, 35*(2), 295–321.

Elsner, J. B., & Jagger, T. H. (2008). Hurricanes and climate change. *Bulletin of the American Meteorological Society, 89*(5), 677–680.

Ely, L. L., Enzel, Y., Baker, V. R., & Cayan, D. R. (1992). A 5000-year record of extreme floods and climate change in the southwestern United States. *Science, 256,* 1434.

Flynn, J., Slovic, P., & Mertz, C. K. (1994). Gender, race, and perception of environmental health risks. *Risk Analysis, 14*(6), 1101–1108.

Fothergill, A., Maestas, E., & Darlington, J. D. (1999). Race, ethnicity and disasters in the United States: A review of the literature. *Disasters, 23*(2), 156–173.

Fothergill, A., & Peek, L. A. (2004). Poverty and disasters in the United States: A review of recent sociological findings. *Natural Hazards, 32*(1), 89–110.

Gladwin, H., & Peacock, W. G. (1997). Warning and evacuation: A night for hard houses. In W. G. Peacock, B. H. Morrow, & H. Gladwin (Eds.), *Hurricane Andrew: Ethnicity, gender and the sociology of disasters.* London: Routledge.

Glick, D. C. (2007). Risk communication for public health emergencies. *Annual Review of Public Health, 28,* 33–54.

Henderson-Sellers, A., Zhang, H., Berz, G., Emmanuel, K., Gray, W., Lansea, C., . . . & McGuffie, K. (1998). Tropical cyclones and global climate change: A post-IPCC assessment. *Bulletin of the American Meteorological Society, 79*(1), 19.

HISTORY.com. *Slavery in America.* Retrieved from www.history.com/topics/black-history/slavery

Karl, T. R., Melillo, J. M., & Peterson, T. C. (Eds.). (2009). *Global climate change impacts in the United States.* Cambridge: Cambridge University Press.

Kasperson, R., Renn, O., Slovik, P., Brown, H. S., Emel, J., Goble, R., & Kasperson, J. X. (1988). The social amplification of risk: A conceptual framework. *Risk Analysis, 8*(2), 177–187.

Klinenberg, E. (2002). *Heat wave: A social autopsy of disaster in Chicago.* Chicago, IL: University of Chicago Press.

Leiss, W., & Powell, D. (1997). *Mad cows and mothers milk.* Montreal: McGill-Queen's Press Montreal Google Scholar.

McMichael, A. J., Woodruff, R. E., & Hales, S. (2006). Climate change and human health: Present and future risks. *The Lancet, 367*(9513), 859–869.

McMichael, A. J., Woodruff, R. E., Whetton, P. R. E., Whetton, P., et al. (2003). *Human health and climate change in Oceania: A risk assessment* (p. 116). Canberra, Australia: Commonwealth Department of Health and Ageing.

Morgan, M. G., Fischoff, B., Bostrom, A., & Atman, C. J. (2002). *Risk communication: A mental models approach.* Cambridge: Cambridge University Press.

Morrow, B. H. (1999). Identifying and mapping community vulnerability. *Disasters, 23*(1), 1–18.

National Academy of Sciences. (2006). *Facing hazards and disasters: Understanding human dimensions.* Committee on Disaster Research in the Social Sciences: Future Challenges and Opportunities. Washington, DC: National Research Council. National Consensus Panel on Emergency.

O'Brien, G., O'Keefe, P., Rose, J., & Wisner, B. (2006). Natural disasters and climate change. *Disasters, 30*(1), 64–80.

Peacock, W. G., & Girard, C. (1997). Ethnic and racial inequalities in hurricane damage and insurance settlements. In *Hurricane Andrew: Ethnicity, gender and the sociology of disasters* (pp. 171–190). London: Routledge.

Peacock, W. G., Morrow, B. H., & Gladwin, H. (Eds.). (1997). *Hurricane Andrew: Ethnicity, gender and the sociology of disasters* (pp. 1–21). London: Routledge.

Rahmstorf, S. (2007). A semi-empirical approach to projecting future sea-level rise. *Science, 315*(5810), 368–370.

Renn, O., & Klinke, A. (2012). Space matters! Impacts for risk governance. In D. Muller-Mahn (Ed.), *The spatial dimension of risk: How geography shapes the emergence of riskscapes.* London, New York: Routledge.

Reuveny, R. (2007). Climate change-induced migration and violent conflict. *Political Geography, 26*(6), 656–673.

Reynolds, B., & Seeger, M. (2005). Crisis and emergency risk communication as an integrative model. *Journal of Health Communication, 10*(1), 43–55.

Rohrmann, B., Wiedemann, P. M., & Stegelmann, H. U. (1990). *Risk communication: An interdisciplinary bibliography.* Programmgruppe Mensch, Umwelt, Technik (MUT) der KFA Jülich.

Rowel, R., Sheikhattari, P., Barber, T., & Evans-Halland, M. (2012). Introduction of a guide to enhance risk communication among low-income and minority populations: A grassroots community engagement approach. *Health Promotion Practice, 13*(1), 124–132.

Schwartz, P., & Randall, D. (2003). *An abrupt climate change scenario and its implications for United States national security.* Pasadena, CA: California Institute of Technology Jet Propulsion Lab.

Spence, P. R., Lachlan, K. A., & Griffin, D. R. (2007). Crisis communication, race, and natural disasters. *Journal of Black Studies, 37*(4), 539–554.

Ulbrich, U., Pinto, J. G., Kupfer, H., Leckebusch, G. C., Spangehl, T., & Reyers, M. (2008). Changing Northern Hemisphere storm tracks in an ensemble of IPCC climate change simulations. *Journal of Climate, 21*(8), 1669–1679.

3 Voices in the garden

Designing social change at the intersection of green radicalism and participatory media

Patrick D. Murphy and Clemencia Rodríguez

Introduction

The fields of communication for social change and environmental communication have both produced deep pools of scholarship and theoretical frameworks essential for guiding our understanding of how community participation and collaborative problem solving can boost social change (e.g., Huesca, 2008; Murphy, 2017; Rodríguez, 2001; Obregón & Tufte, 2017; Sandler & Pezzullo, 2007; Waisbord, 2008). Both fields have also evolved over the years to offer various prescriptions for engendering human agency that privilege consciousness-raising through discovery, self-representation, voice, and cultural experience. Yet despite these shared points of emphasis and their potential to inform progressive social change, the two traditions have tended to float free from one another and are rarely put in dialogue. The project detailed in this chapter is an attempt to correct this disconnection – or at least offer an example of one way to approach bridging this divide – through a community centered eco-pedagogy project still in its nascent stages. The project, implemented in a predominantly African-American community in Philadelphia, intends to use participatory media to engage youth and children with urban green spaces. Drawing on notions of citizenship, voice, and political agency shared by green radicalism and participatory media, the project's goal is to trigger awareness around environmental issues and the importance of green spaces in urban communities as a first step toward green consciousness.

The chapter begins with an explication of green radicalism, an approach to environmental activism that combines green consciousness with social justice. We emphasize the concept of "voice" as central to green radicalism, and as a gateway for thinking about ways of linking Communication for Social Change and Environmental Communication. Voice is also a central concept within the theory and practice of participatory media, thus we position it as the starting point from which to think and act at the intersection of environmental communication and communication for social change. The chapter then explores central concepts of participatory media, a vital subfield within the theory, research, and action of communication for social change and one that is deeply connected with the appropriation of media technologies and social justice issues.

The final part of the chapter is dedicated to describing *Urban Green Spaces and Digital Technologies*, the title we have given to a "green" social change community initiative started in 2017 that combines principles from environmental communication with practices of participatory media. The goal of this initiative is to use media technologies and digital platforms to connect young people to local green spaces in Philadelphia's low-income communities. The project is designed on the assumption that if youth are given the opportunity to process their experiences in local green spaces through the storytelling potential of media technologies, they will make connections between environmental issues and social justice. The setting for this project is Philadelphia, Pennsylvania, and, as explicated in greater detail below, it involves three primary stakeholders within the northern part of the city: Temple University's Klein College of Media and Communication; the Village of the Arts and the Humanities, a grassroots community organization; and La Finquita, an urban farm in danger of being swallowed by gentrification. The project is in its early phases and evaluation is still preliminary.

Green radicalism

Green radicalism is a discourse within contemporary environmentalism that is associated with a wide range of ideologies and environmental action movements, particularly those that situate themselves against the status quo (Dryzek, 2013; Stevenson, 2014). Broadly speaking, green radicalism is a progressive, action-oriented discourse animated by the goal of creating a green public sphere through confronting recalcitrant practices and transforming the institutions and thinking that support them through resistance and alternative activities. Green radicalism has been characterized as a discursive practice of self-authorized representation constructed to make claims that put into question the role of traditional authority (e.g., the state), seeking out instead a fundamental reorientation through alternative visions of existence tied to social justice, human rights, and/or the rights of nature (Stevenson, 2014). Movements and ideologies aligned with it include, among others, environmental justice, a movement focused on environmental risk, particularly as it affects ethnic minorities and the poor; and ecological citizenship, a green philosophy that defines citizen rights and responsibilities in relation to environmental stewardship and obligations to future generations.

In his seminal work, *The Politics of the Earth*, John Dryzek (2013) divides green radicalism into two identifiable traditions: green politics, which focuses on changing social structures, and green consciousness, which is driven by changing the way people think. For the purposes of the *Urban Green Spaces and Digital Technologies* initiative, both traditions are pertinent, especially because the two trajectories of green radicalism show signs of merging. For instance, historically the green politics efforts of green radicalism in marginalized communities have been directly tied to environmental justice. In the 1970s and 80s, the links between marginalization and environmental risk became increasingly salient through the racial, social, and economic factors implicated by the prevalence of toxic industrial waste dumps in poor and ethnic minority communities throughout the United States. As the unequal distribution of environmental threats experienced by minority and low-income communities became better understood, so did the degree to which those communities began to engage in struggles for recognition, political agency, and environmental rights. The grassroots movements led by people of color and working class communities redefined the environment "to encompass where we live, work, play, and learn – and some add where we pray, to include, for example, indigenous sacred sites and Appalachian graveyards" (Pezzullo & Cox, 2018, p. 258).

By 1980, the Superfund Law (or more formally, Comprehensive Environmental Response, Compensation, and Liability Act) was established to clean-up contaminated sites that endangered public health. Not long after, the "idea of the environmental justice movement burst into view of the American consciousness in 1982 when there were more than 500 arrests in the largely African-American community of Afton, North Carolina, during a campaign of nonviolent civil disobedience directed toward preventing the disposal of PBC-laced soil in the Warren County landfill" (Jamieson, 2007, p. 88). This law, and the subsequent movement, precipitated an increase in localized activism, altering the terrain of the environmental movement in a way that thereafter made it necessary to account for issues of human rights and social justice (Sandler & Pezzullo, 2007).

Since these foundational moments, there has been a lively and continuing debate about how environmental justice is defined and whose interests it represents, but at its core it can be understood simply by the assertion that "all people and communities are entitled to equal protection of environmental and public health, laws and regulations" (Bullard, 1996, p. 493). As a movement, it has been described as "dedicated to justice in the distribution of environmental goods and decision making" (Sandler & Pezzullo, 2007, p. 1). As these definitions underscore, the central concern of environmental justice is the struggle for recognition and political agency enmeshed in issues of risk, pollution, protection, health, and sustainability.

This turn toward struggle and agency has meant that "voice" and "human rights" have become part of the language of environmentalism, signaling a fuller appreciation for how people's storylines, particularly marginalized people's storylines, are recognized in relation to the natural world.

Unlike green politics, green consciousness has been much less associated with the more confrontational activities of environmental justice. "Thinking green" does not have a history of the sort of "image events" (boycotts, protests, sit-ins) that "make the invisible matter" in relation to the environmental rights of disempowered communities (DeLuca, 2006). Nevertheless, the "green consciousness" aspects of environmental justice loom large even if they have tended to be largely untapped.

There are signs that this is beginning to change, with a grafting together of notions of environmental citizenship with environmental justice. One of the more visible signs of change is the ascension of Aaron Mair as the first African-American to serve as the President of the Sierra Club (2015–2017). John Muir, a patron saint of American environmentalism and a staunch preservationist, founded the Sierra Club in 1892. Following Muir, for much of its history the Sierra Club remained focused on wilderness issues. Through his various leadership positions in the Sierra Club, Mair has consistently pushed the organization to focus on environmental justice, asserting that modern environmentalists must be deeply aware of how the intersections of race, culture, and politics inform the exercise of power (Mair, 2017). Within this context, "voice" and the "politics of place" have moved beyond the discursive fields of green radicalism to take up a much more prominent place within the contours of contemporary environmentalism.

Participatory media

The 1968 publication of Paulo Freire's *Pedagogía do Oprimido* (Pedagogy of the Oppressed) in Brazil marked the emergence of a new way of thinking about language and power. Freire saw a clear link between power and issues of voice. According to Freire (1968), the impact of poverty, injustice, and oppression extends well beyond issues of access to material resources, plunging individuals and communities into states of isolation and what he calls "a culture of silence." People without access to power lose their own voices and learn to mimic the voice of the powerful. Freire advocated a critical and empowering approach to education that could break through the culture of silence; he thought that people would be able to overcome processes of alienation, isolation, and silence by insisting on appropriating their own language and learning new ways "to speak to the world."

For Freire, dialogue and interaction are essential to these processes. It is through dialogue and interaction with others that a person can move from being "a passive object of others" to being a subject and an individual with agency. In this sense, "voice" implies having access to the necessary language tools to interpret the world in which one lives; having access to the means to position one's articulations of the world in the public sphere; and having the ability to transform language into action. Voice is language, agency, and, ultimately, political power.

Since Freire's ground-breaking ideas appeared, the field of alternative media and participatory communication has aspired to explore and analyze how media appropriation processes are linked to empowerment and agency. Media technologies are particularly interesting because they facilitate processes of language appropriation. Learning to operate a video camera and capturing the images and sounds in one's environment is an exercise in appropriating audiovisual languages. Learning to edit sound and image or to distribute one's own narratives via social media is all about language appropriation and the dissemination of one's own voice. Using a microphone to capture the sounds of everyday life and community is an exercise in agency; a discerning subject has to continually make decisions about which sounds to privilege, which ones to disregard, and how to narrate the immediate social and natural universe. Media technologies exist precisely to capture raw experience and transform it into narrative and, in that capacity, they offer exceptional potential for the development of voice, agency, and empowerment – the main components of what Freire called "conscientization."

Deeply influenced by Freire's notions of power and language, Colombian media scholar Clemencia Rodríguez advanced the field of participatory media research with a series of ethnographic studies of community media in Latin America. Drawing from her field data and Chantal Mouffe's (1988, 1992a, 1992b) theories of democracy and citizenship, Rodríguez (2001) coined the term "citizens' media" to refer to alternative, community, or radical media that facilitate, trigger, and maintain processes of building citizenship, as it is defined by Mouffe.

Breaking away from liberal theories of democracy that define citizenship as a status granted to the individual by the state, Mouffe proposed a radically different notion of citizenship as enacted political agency in local spheres. In other words, Mouffe's citizen is an individual who continuously enacts their agency, changing and shaping the local community according to personal notions of "what ought to be." Rodríguez' "citizens' media" are those media that promote symbolic processes that allow communities to appropriate languages to name the world in their own terms, narrate their identities, express their own visions for the future, and ultimately shape and change their own communities. Here, Rodríguez connects with Jesús Martín Barbero's theories of identity, language, and political power. According to Martín Barbero (2002), the power of communities to name the world in their own terms is directly linked with their power to enact political actions. Martín Barbero plays with a linguistic pun on the Spanish terms "*contar*" (to narrate) and "*contar*" (to have a strong presence, to count) and explains that only those who can "*contar*" (narrate) will "*contar*" – meaning that only those with the ability to narrate their own identities and name the world in their own terms will have a strong presence as political subjects.

According to Rodríguez (2001), "citizens' media" are those media that facilitate the transformation of individuals and communities into Mouffe's "citizens" and Martín Barbero's powerful subjectivities with a voice. Citizens' media are communication spaces in which adults and children learn to manipulate their languages, codes, signs, and symbols, gaining power to name the world. Citizens' media trigger processes that allow individuals and communities to re-codify their contexts and selves. These processes ultimately give citizens the opportunity to re-structure their identities into empowered subjectivities strongly connected to local cultures and driven by well-defined utopias. Citizens' media are the media citizens use to activate communication processes that shape their local communities. In this sense, citizens' media are media for social change.

The concept of citizens' media has been used by other scholars to analyze participatory media initiatives in different parts of the world. Based on an in-depth visual ethnography of women in Fiji, Usha Harris (2008) demonstrated how participatory video could trigger multiple social and cultural processes that enhance women's empowerment and cultural/social capital. Harris's work supports the idea that, as marginalized people learn to produce their own media content and master media technologies, a series of processes of appropriation, voice, self-expression, and ultimately empowerment take place. In similar research, Heather Anderson documented processes of media technology appropriation and empowerment among prisoners (2012). Based on four case studies in Australia and Canada, Anderson's research demonstrates that appropriation of media technologies – in this case radio – triggers transformative processes in some of the most isolated and silenced communities.

In geographic locations as different as New York City in the Global North, Medellín, Colombia (an urban metropolis in the Global South), and a small town in the Colombian Amazon, youth media initiatives enable processes of voice and empowerment through participatory media making. For example, in low-income neighborhoods in Medellín, Colombia, a local non-profit called *Pasolini en Medellín* (PeM) uses participatory filmmaking and visual ethnography to immerse people in processes that destabilize mainstream media narratives. PeM was founded in 2008 by two young local filmmakers committed to social change in their neighborhoods. During the

1980s and 1990s, Medellín's marginalized neighborhoods became the battleground of drug lords, paramilitary groups, leftist guerrillas, and territorial gangs (Riaño-Alcalá, 2006). These neighborhoods, known as *comunas*, are some of the most stigmatized places on earth. National and international media only report from these neighborhoods when drug mafias wreak havoc or when the police and the army try to impose their military might on *comunas*. Mainstream media narratives such as *Narcos* construct *comunas* as places where everyone is armed and only war and violence exist. It is in these same *comunas* that PeM opened its doors to community members, offering a media pedagogy specifically designed to invite residents to re-signify the world around them. First-time participants were asked to keep field diaries that make the familiar strange:

> Sounds of my neighborhood: Brushing, sneezing, blender, chickens, cough, phlegm, the screaming cooking pot, washing clothes, snoring, dishes, pigs, cries, bikes, the metro, urination, refrigerator, iron, sex, groans, the creek, bathing, death and its mourning, flush the toilet, football, belching, babies, weekends, yawning.
>
> (Carlos Santos's field diary in Perez Quintero, 2013, p. 69).

Inspired by Italian filmmaker Pier Paolo Pasolini's notion of the need to "poetize reality" in the slums of Rome, PeM's media production workshops also include tasting, listening, viewing, feeling, mapping, and walking exercises. The experience of observing the world through a cardboard frame makes a strong impression on participating youth:

> The exercises with the cardboard frame, uff!, that really changed my life! We looked through the cardboard frames at our church, our block, or my dog, which is also a main character in all of our stories.
>
> (Benítez in Perez Quintero, 2013, p. 74)

PeM believes that media should allow people to re-signify themselves, their reality, and their experience. In Medellín's neighborhoods, where war has imposed meanings, ways of understanding, and cultural codes on daily life, PeM youth participants use cameras and microphones to produce narratives that show their neighborhood in a very different way. Countering stigmatized versions of their neighborhoods, PeM filmmakers create narratives that capture their lived experiences growing up in *comunas*. PeM's videos show these neighborhoods as complex communities where people love, create, enjoy, work, and play. The notion of voice is at the center of PeM's mission. The appropriation of media is, PeM believes, the first step toward politically active subjects.

In Southern Colombia, the Escuela Audivisual Infantil de Belén de los Andaquíes (EAIBA) [Children's Audiovisual School] involves children and youth in playful processes of media production and storytelling. The motto of the school, "Without a Story, There's No Camera," emphasizes the privileging of storytelling over technology. Technology is only useful if it enables the translation of local voices, local aesthetics, and local languages into media products to be shared in the public sphere. EAIBA involves children and youth in a media pedagogy centered on re-evaluating self and place. EAIBA immerses children and youth in participatory media production processes in which microphones and viewfinders are used to capture local sounds and images and encourage children to use their own voices and their own local ways of speaking and interpreting reality to re-signify what they see and hear (Pérez Quintero, Ramírez, & Rodríguez, 2015; Rodríguez, 2011, Chapter 1). The North Philadelphia neighborhood where the *Urban Green Spaces and Digital Technologies* is located experiences similar levels of stigmatization. For decades, media narratives have promoted the notion that North Philadelphia is a place of gun violence, urban blight, poverty, and marginalization. In the imagination of Philadelphians, North Philly exists as a threatening place to be avoided.

In New York City, Global Action Project (GAP) (http://global-action.org/) engages youth in participatory media processes to foster community power, cultural expression, and political change. Diana Coryat's evaluation study on GAP demonstrates that media making not only empowers children and youth to speak with their own voices, but it also triggers youth involvement in civic engagement and social justice movements. According to Coryat, GAP participants learned to "re/read and re/write their subject positions . . . to see themselves as change agents in society" and "began to conceive and enact their citizenship differently" (Coryat, 2014, p. 177). Coryat's research subjects explain how participatory media production engaged them in re-examining daily life as highly political and linked to global and national economic and political structures, to human rights issues, and to social change. Once they began seeing the quotidian as political, GAP's young participants began to explore ways to become politically active in social movements and other types of activist initiatives.

A robust body of research demonstrates that participatory media processes lead to voice, political agency, and youth empowerment. When well designed, participatory media initiatives facilitate access to the technological capacity to produce, express, and distribute meaning – the conditions of voice. As young participants internalize the expertise to playfully create their own meaning, a series of transformations follow, including self-trust, civic engagement, decreased inhibitions, and a general feeling of being able to intervene and transform one's social reality.

Working at the intersection of green radicalism and participatory media

Green radicalism advocates for an eco-consciousness that empowers individuals and communities to question the injustices linked to environmental degradation and learn to navigate the obstacles they impose. The field of participatory media has accumulated a robust portfolio of media pedagogy initiatives and research that demonstrate the empowering potential of language appropriation that comes with media production. To echo Freire, through an insistence on helping communities appropriate their own language and learn new ways "to speak the world," participatory media, coupled with the eco-pedagogy of green radicalism, can be a means to trigger political agency. Our challenge was to design a communication for social change initiative that would combine these two pools of thought and action. Our initiative needed to dip into the potential of storytelling and the use of media technologies proposed by participatory media. It also needed to delve into the linkages and articulations between environmental elements and social justice and ultimately, it should bring agency and empowerment to our neighbor community in North Philly.

The neighborhood

North Philadelphia is a term generally used by outsiders to refer to an area of the city that includes several different unique and distinct neighborhoods. The term "North Philly" erases specificities and emphasizes a few characteristics these neighborhoods have in common: they are comprised mostly of ethnic minority communities, mainly African-American and Latino; they are low-income communities; and they experience high levels of violence, poverty, and marginalization. For local residents, then, "North Philly" is not self-ascribed, but stems from outsiders' perceptions of these neighborhoods, an attitude that combines stigma and ignorance. Locals tend to not use the term "North Philly," and instead refer to the specific neighborhood names, such as Germantown, Nicetown, Badlands, Fishtown, El Centro de Oro, to name but a few. The community that hosts the Village of the Arts and Humanities, home of the *Urban Green Spaces and Digital Technologies* initiative, is known as Fairhill.

Due to its proximity to the Delaware River, the northeast section of the city was once one of the most important manufacturing hubs in the country. Key landmarks, such as the Craven and Dearnley Mill and the Grand Opera House are reminders of the high manufacturing days of the city. Craven and Dearnley Mill was once an important manufacturing company employing close to 500 Philadelphians. The Grand Opera House on Broad and

Montgomery, less than a mile from the Mill, operated from 1888 to 1940. By 1935, 40% of the buildings in this section in the northeast of Philadelphia were factories (Sicotte & Swanson, 2007, p. 519).

During this time, the city was home to many large manufacturing companies, but the great majority of manufacturing jobs were found in small companies, workshops, and factories that employed a quarter of a million workers and traded with each other, making the city a tight network of manufacturing and trade: "carpet makers purchased yarn from one firm, had it dyed at a second, bought pattern designs from a third, punched cards to control the weaving process (Jacquard) from a fourth" (Scranton, 1990).

In sharp contrast with the ethnic profile of this neighborhood today, in 1935, 85% of the residents were of British and German descent; residents lived and worked in close proximity, a result of urban planning that concentrated factory structures and low-income row homes in the same neighborhoods (Sicotte & Swanson, 2007, p. 520).

Philadelphia experienced during the second half of the 20th century the demise of its manufacturing industry: "the Philadelphia Naval Shipyard closed down in 1995 after 194 years of business. At the end of the 1920s, the city's largest employers, Baldwin Locomotive, the Frankford Arsenal, Mid Vale Steel and others underwent massive layoffs, merely setting the stage for full closures years later" (Kostelni, 2000, p. 20). By the late 1950s, Philadelphia's northeast had lost most of its manufacturing to foreign imports; white residents moved to the suburbs as African-Americans moved from the traditional black neighborhoods in south Philly to the northeast. According to census data, only 7.6% of the neighborhood labor force of today works in manufacturing. The 1960s was a time of gentrification and urban renewal in the center and south of the city, which displaced even more African-Americans to the northeast neighborhoods (Sicotte & Swanson, 2007, p. 521).

According to the 2010 census data, Fairhill is home to 26,000 residents: 41% African-American and 23% White. Almost 60% of the neighborhood residents identify as Latino (59.7%), including various races (White Latino, Black Latino, other Latino) and origins (51.5% Puerto Rican, 1.7% Mexican, and 6% other Latino/Hispanic). In terms of family profiles, 41.4% of the households are woman-only households and 44% have children living in them. According to census data estimates from 2016, the unemployment rate in the neighborhood is 23.8%, more than double that of the country; 30.6% earn less than $10,000/year, and 18.7% earn less than $25,000/year. More than half (52%) of the neighborhood families live below the poverty line and 70% of all children under 18 live below the poverty line. Predictably, the neighborhood's level of educational achievement is low, with close to 30% of all adults 25 years or older having less than a high school education.

The Fairhill community has endured the various forces that push low-income urban neighborhoods into alienation: poverty, unemployment, low educational achievement, racial inequality, and gentrification. The neighborhood is also situated in one of Philadelphia's most "extensively burdened" environmental riskscapes, with dangers that include hazardous waste and the clustering of closed factories, power plants, and waste facilities, along with other markers of environmental injustice, such as abandoned lots and lack of green spaces (Sicotte, 2010). However, poverty, exclusion, and environmental risk do not exhaust the meaning of this community. At its heart is a commercial district abundant with signs of community revitalization, such as a community job training center, accessible public waste and recycling bins, and a rise in local entrepreneurship. A massive splash of color frames this commercial corridor in the form of a two block mural art project developed by Dutch artists Dre Urhahn and Jeroen Koolhaas (better known as Haas and Hahn) in collaboration with local youth. In a style similar to Haas and Hahn's famous mural in the Santa Marta favela in Rio de Janeiro, the mural on Germantown Avenue covers 50 individual buildings with bright colors in stark contrast with the gray shapes of the surrounding urban environment.

The university

Located in North Philadelphia, Temple University is a public research institution with a history of serving as a resource for local residents, who historically have been working class. Russell Conwell, its founder and first president, had an impassioned commitment to serving the local community and this commitment remains celebrated within Temple lore, but many of the surrounding communities, most of which are low-income neighborhoods inhabited mostly by ethnic minorities, feel that today Temple does little for North Philadelphia.

Under new leadership, Temple University's Klein College of Media and Communication has revised its mission toward a general focus on urban communication, and, with Temple's Conwellian roots in mind, the University is trying to correct this disconnect by seeking out ways to productively engage with local social actors. The Klein College sees this role as vital, as the North Philadelphia setting presents an emblematic case of the marginalization and abandonment that global neo-liberal economic models have brought to large American cities.

As detailed in the previous section, economic policies driven by global actors stripped working class neighborhoods from their manufacturing base, creating harsh economic conditions for the communities that provided an abundance of manufacturing labor from the late 1800s to the 1980s.

Moreover, as also already alluded to, Philadelphia is one of the nation's most industrially polluted cities, with poorer communities being disproportionately burdened with environmental hazards (Sicotte, 2010). In this context and given the university's resources, the Klein College has the responsibility to re-think how to put communication and media at the service of its neighbors, privileging research, teaching, and outreach initiatives that involve working with the communities of North Philadelphia. The *Urban Green Spaces and Digital Technologies* project is one of these community outreach initiatives.

The community center

The Village of the Arts and Humanities, a grassroots community center that has operated in Fairhill since the 1970s, has a long history of deep connections with the local context and it is viewed with high levels of respect and legitimacy by community members. The center was created to engage children and youth in art and media practices to foster creative and critical skills, build potential for personal success, and strengthen a sense of belonging to local communities. The Village includes a "Creative Impacts Studio" art education program and "PhillyEarth," an environmental education and urban farming program; both of these programs provide a rich framework for a digital humanities initiative. These activities and services have been instrumental in the local community's resuscitation.

To expand its operations, the Village recently purchased two old buildings, one of which was being used for the sale of alcohol, and planned to turn them into campus facilities. So, while it is clear that the community continues to face many challenges, the neighborhood also offers signs of resilience, solidarity, and community engagement and the Village is a central protagonist in these narratives.

The garden

With help from the Pennsylvania Horticultural Society, which operates almost 500 community gardens in the city of Philadelphia as part of its "Community Gardens" program, as well as a shared food program, a "Roots to Reentry" prison horticultural program, and a "Clean and Green" community landscaping program that transforms vacant land into open spaces for communities, *Urban Green Spaces* was presented with the opportunity to work with "La Finquita," an urban farm/community garden located in the South Kensington district of Philadelphia.

La Finquita means "The Small Farm" in Spanish, reflecting the Latino origins of the garden. Established on an owner-abandoned lot, the then-Latino residents of the neighborhood began farming on this property in 1988. Produce includes corn, spinach, squash, broccoli, onions, eggplant, green peppers, and more, and the gardeners also practice beekeeping and composting. Volunteer members operate a produce stand on Sundays, offering the local community fresh produce at a very reasonable price. Today, as the result of the encroachment of gentrification from nearby neighborhoods, a new wave of members have joined ranks with some of the founding volunteers. Gardening in La Finquita has become more diverse. In terms of age, an older generation in their 50s and 60s works shoulder to shoulder with a generation of young adults beginning their professional careers in the tech world or still in graduate school. With the exception of a few toddlers, currently there are no youth members.

Recently, the question of the lot's ownership has surfaced, greatly threatening La Finquita's future. Myrone LLC, a real estate developer, noticed that La Finquita sits on the frontier between the highly gentrified neighborhood of Northern Liberties and the still depressed area known as Old Kensington. La Finquita is located exactly one block north of the northern boundary of Northern Liberties. The lot located next to La Finquita was developed in 2017 by a real estate company; each of the seven "boutique townhouses" built next to La Finquita are going on the market in 2018 for approximately $500,000 each.

According to La Finquita volunteer gardeners, Myrone LLC searched for the heirs of Pyramid Tire and Rubber Co, La Finquita's lot's original owner, until they were found in a different part of the country. The heirs accepted the Myrone's proposal to pay all the unpaid taxes to the city, and received another $90,000 in compensation for the lot.

To avoid eviction from the lot, La Finquita gardeners took the case to court. Claiming squatter's rights, which protect the right to property when it has been occupied for more than 20 years, La Finquita volunteers claimed legal rights over the lot. On March 16, 2018, La Finquita settled the case with Myrone for a significant payment (for more information on the court case see www.pubintlaw.org/cases-and-projects/la-finquita-community-farm/).

La Finquita's plight is a textbook case of gentrification violently intruding to disrupt local processes of resistance in low-income urban environments. Across the street from La Finquita sits a large building, originally an umbrella factory, now undergoing major construction. A developer is renovating the building, rescuing its old charm and transforming it into large loft condos for rent. At La Finquita, rumors circulate that rent prices will be on the high end, at $1,400 a month for a studio apartment; everyone at La Finquita is outraged at the cost. A few blocks away, at 1700 5th Street, another large factory building, another reminder of the area's manufacturing past, has already been renovated and transformed into expensive rentals; the sign on the front door reads: "Lamp Factory – Loft Apartments."

The initiative

Funded by Temple's Humanities and Arts Program Award, we conceptualized the *Urban Green Spaces and Digital Technologies* project as a "green" social change community initiative that would involve multiple local partners invested in progressive, sustainable change within the city. Apart from the conceptual frameworks provided by green radicalism and participatory media, we could now count on a partnership with the Village of the Arts and Humanities and the connection to La Finquita, made possible by a partnership with the Pennsylvania Horticultural Society. The Village, with its after-school and summer programs for children and youth, provided an ideal structure for implementing a child and youth-centered initiative designed around the notion of voice. The project seeks to harness the storytelling potential of media technologies and encourage involvement with environmental issues through urban green spaces to activate processes of voice, agency, and empowerment.

The City of Philadelphia has developed a robust number of environmentally friendly initiatives including collective gardens, urban agriculture, composting facilities, and pollution elimination strategies (such as using plants to clean lead from soils). However, these green initiatives engage mostly older citizens while local youth remain indifferent, rarely showing interest in participating and engaging with the creation and maintenance of green spaces in their local neighborhoods. Drawing from the participatory media models developed in the field of citizens' media studies (Rodríguez, 2001) and the call for social justice environmentalism found in green radicalism (Dryzek, 2013; Stevenson, 2014), we designed a community engagement project conceptualized as an intervention through media and digital platforms to encourage children and youth to participate in establishing and sustaining local urban green spaces. The field of participatory media research has greatly advanced our understanding of media making as complex processes that trigger profound transformative processes. Meanwhile, the progressive characteristics of green radicalism suggest ways for community-based environmentalism to engender environmental citizenship while pursuing questions of environmental justice. The project's goal is to use media technologies and digital platforms to connect young people to local green spaces in a low-income community in North Philadelphia. The project is driven by three core elements: 1) an environmental element in the form of urban green spaces; 2) a media element in the form of photography and video; and 3) a digital element in the form of geo-mapping and a web portal. The Village of the Arts and Humanities provided a base of operations and recruited ten local youth as project participants.

After an initial phase of basic training, slated to begin in spring 2018, our young participants will document their local green spaces using photography, video, and geo-mapping. Led by project coordinators, the youth will photograph, video record, and map La Finquita. Shadowing knowledgeable and committed older gardeners, the young people will document seasonal transitions, following the gardening process from the preparation of the soil and the planting in early spring through the weeding and harvesting in the summer. In the final stage, the participants will produce visual and digital documentation organized into an interactive digital portal focused on local community gardens in Philadelphia. The central notion behind the project is that in cases where young urbanites are not interested in gardening and do not value green spaces, we can interpellate them through media and digital platforms. In other words, if urban green spaces do not draw young people on their own, the challenge of photographing and video recording what happens in those green spaces could be an alternative path toward green consciousness and valuing green spaces in low-income urban environments. At a practical level we wanted to shift the gaze toward those social and cultural spaces where nature still thrives in the midst of urban landscapes scarred by environmental degradation.

We designed *Urban Green Spaces and Digital Technologies* to bring the transformative potential of participatory media and the progressive, eco-conscious elements of green radicalism to multiple stakeholders within the Fairhill community and, eventually, other communities within North Philadelphia. The intended outcomes include:

1) Increased youth engagement with urban green spaces.
2) Increased awareness of environmental sustainability, food security, climate change, and the significance of green spaces in urban environments among local youth.
3) Enhanced skills in photography, video, and web design among the participants.
4) Increased cross-generational communication and sharing of knowledge.
5) A group of trained local youth capable of training a subsequent group during a second phase of the project (a process known as "training for trainers").
6) A collection of photographs and videos about local community gardens, produced by local youth.
7) An interactive portal devoted to community gardens that includes photographs, videos, and geo-mapping.

The *Urban Green Spaces and Digital Technologies* project intends to bring Fairhill youth to La Finquita; to trigger processes of empowerment and agency through media appropriation; and to promote green conscious-ness, the appreciation of urban green spaces, and intergenerational knowl-edge sharing. This initiative brings together three different organizations – a public university, an urban farm, and a community organization – in what we hope will become a long-term collaborative relationship.

Final notes: getting started

A pilot version of the *Urban Green Spaces and Digital Technologies* project was run in 2017. Despite a series of challenges caused by the usual discon-nections and miscommunications that plague projects that include multiple partners, several youth went through weeks of training in media making. A small group of African-American boys and girls, aged 14–16, met weekly at the Village for a few hours of media making training. Some of that time they traveled to La Finquita with their cameras and microphones to connect with the farmers and capture cultivation practices, crop development, beekeep-ing, the sale of the harvest, and any other happenings in this urban garden.

It is far too early to assess profound issues of voice and empowerment in this pilot. However, in the form of preliminary findings we can say that the children are being "seduced" by this green space. We have witnessed moments in which the children express discomfort at having to walk in a muddy environment, resenting having dirt on their good sneakers, having to coexist with bugs, and being denied the comfort of air conditioning dur-ing hot and humid summer sessions. And yet, we also witnessed moments in which the children were captivated by the garden. On a sweaty afternoon toward the end of the summer, one of the children followed a large butter-fly flying around the beds dedicated to the cultivation of flowers. The boy sprung into action to video record and/or photograph the butterfly in flight. Easier said than done. The boy tried to capture it with his camera, but the butterfly was never still. He had a hard time, but he continued his attempts. He tried to get a girl, another participant, excited about the butterfly, but she was too busy putting on bug spray. The boy exclaimed: "But look at it, it is majestic!"

Here, we can begin to see glimpses of "voice." The boy's expression is directly connected to his experience in the local green space. The garden has engendered a new experience, and the boy finds a way to transform that experience into language. Also, the butterfly stands very far from the usual tropes used to describe the urban environment in North Philadelphia. A majestic butterfly in an urban farm is not how the media usually portray these neighborhoods. The boy and his camera stray away from traditional media narratives to begin a process of re-calibrating the senses, reframing social reality, and re-signifying the world around him.

Here we can also see some signs of how experiences in green places serve to facilitate a greening of consciousness and an appreciation for green spaces. The productive discomfort of moving through these places, capturing their sights and sounds, but also experiencing the visceral aspects of "being there" (smells, tastes, feelings) underscores how the process of discovery can serve as a form of eco-pedagogy. The power of the embodied experience within a garden of emerging, growing, and transforming life in contrast to a cityscape otherwise defined by decay and neglect can seed not only an appreciation for green spaces, but also an acknowledgement of their absolute necessity for urban dwellers. In short, access to green spaces can be understood, as green radicalism would frame it, as a human right, not just a luxury for those who live in wealthier parts of the city. Under the conditions created by *Urban Green Spaces and Digital Technologies*, participating youth had access to the lived experience of a green space; the project pushed the kids to go beyond being in the garden toward making sense of the experience and transforming it into camera shots, angles, and movements.

Transforming lived experiences of environmental issues into meaningful narratives is what constitutes a bridge between green consciousness and participatory media. As the kids engage in processes by which they re-signify their reality based on their own experience, they enact their own voice, their own version of things, or as Nick Couldry would say, the kids are "giving an account of themselves" (Couldry, 2010, p. 8). Green consciousness and participatory media intersect precisely here, on the concept of voice, as a fundamental building-block of political agency and democratic life. Voice is a right, a platform to agency, but at the same time it is a resource denied to marginalized communities. *Urban Green Spaces and Digital Technologies* synergized the potential of media appropriation central to participatory media with the notion of environmental justice, understood as marginalized people's storylines about the natural world.

Importantly, the lens of the camera and the capturing of sounds by microphone can help to make this eco-conscious awakening tied to a fuller sense of community, resource stewardship, and multigenerational knowledge, making the site of the garden and the media tools for storytelling devices for environmental justice. This, in turn could lead to a deeper sense of how the community has faced injustices linked to environmental degradation, and how participatory media as a form of social action could be used to confront these community-based issues, engendering a sense of local politics dually grounded in social justice and environmental citizenship.

References

Anderson, H. (2012). *Raising the civil dead: Prisoners and community radio.* New York, NY: Peter Lang.

Bullard, R. D. (1996). Environmental justice: It's more than waste facility siting. *Social Science Quarterly, 77*(3), 493–499.

Coryat, D. (2014). *Critical youth media pedagogy: A case study of global action project.* Saarbrücken, Germany: LAP LAMBERT Academic Publishing.

Couldry, N. (2010). *Why voice matters: Culture and politics after neoliberalism.* London: Sage.

DeLuca, K. (2006). *Image politics: The new rhetoric of environmental activism.* Mahwah, NJ: Erlbaum.

Dryzek, J. S. (2013). *The politics of the earth: Environmental discourses* (3rd ed.). Oxford: Oxford University Press.

Freire, P. (1968). *Pedagogía do Oprimido.* Rio de Janeiro: Paz e Terra.

Harris, U. S. (2008). Video for empowerment and social change. In E. Papoutsaki & U. Sundar Harris (Eds.), *South Pacific Islands communication: Regional perspectives, local issues.* Singapore, Suva, and Auckland: Asian Media Information and Communication Centre (AMIC).

Huesca, R. (2008). Tracing the history of participatory communication approaches to development: A critical appraisal. In J. Servaes (Ed.), *Communication for development and social change.* Thousand Oaks, CA: SAGE.

Jamieson, D. (2007). Justice: The heart of environmentalism. In R. L. Sandler & P. C. Pezzullo (Eds.), *Environmental justice and environmentalism: The social justice challenge to the environmental movement.* Cambridge, MA: MIT Press.

Kostelni, N. (2000). The death of manufacturing. *The Philadelphia Business Journal, 18*(48), 20.

Mair, A. (2017, April 8). *Just transitions: Communication power in the era of climatic change.* Keynote Lecture, Waterhouse Family Institute Symposium 2017, Villanova University.

Martín Barbero, J. (2002). Identities: Traditions and new communities. *Media Culture and Society, 24*(5), 621–641.

Mouffe, C. (1988). Hegemony and new political subjects: Towards a new conception of democracy. In Grossberg & C. Nelson (Eds.), *Marxism and the interpretation of culture.* Urbana, IL and Chicago, IL: University of Illinois Press.

Mouffe, C. (1992a). Democratic citizenship and the political community. In C. Mouffe (Ed.), *Dimensions of radical democracy: Pluralism, citizenship, community.* London: Verso.

Mouffe, C. (1992b). Feminism, citizenship and radical democratic politics. In J. Buttler & J. W. Scott (Eds.), *Feminists theorize the political.* New York, NY: Routledge.

Murphy, P. (2017). *The media commons: Globalization and environmental discourses.* Urbana, IL: University of Illinois Press.

Obregón, R., & Tufte, T. (2017). Communication, social movements, and collective action: Toward a new research agenda in communication for development and social change. *Journal of Communication, 67*(5), 635–645.

Perez Quintero, C. E. (2013). Images to Disarm Minds: An Exploration of the "Pasolini en Medellin" Experience in Colombia (Doctoral dissertation, Ohio University).

Pérez Quintero, C., Ramírez, C., & Rodríguez, C. (2015). Cameras and stories to disarm wars: Performative communication in alternative media. In C. Atton (Ed.), *The Routledge companion to alternative and community media*. London: Routledge.

Pezzullo, P. C., & Cox, R. (2018). *Environmental communication and the public sphere* (5th ed.). Los Angeles, CA: SAGE.

Riaño-Alcalá, P. (2006). *Dwellers of memory: Youth and violence in Medellin, Colombia*. Piscataway, NJ: Transaction Publishers.

Rodríguez, C. (2001). *Fissures in the mediascape: An international study of Citizens' media*. Newbury Park, CA: Hampton Press.

Rodríguez, C. (2011). *Citizens' media against armed conflict: Disrupting violence in Colombia*. Minneapolis, MN: University of Minnesota Press.

Sandler, R. L., & Pezzullo, P. C. (Eds.). (2007). *Environmental justice and environmentalism: The social justice challenge to the environmental movement*. Cambridge, MA: MIT Press.

Scranton, P. (1990). *Philadelphia: The world's greatest workshop*. Retrieved November 10, 2017 from www.workshopoftheworld.com/overview/overview.html.

Sicotte, D. (2010). Some more polluted that others: Unequal cumulative industrial hazard burdens in the Philadelphia MSA, USA. *Local Environment, 15*(8), 761–774.

Sicotte, D., & Swanson, S. (2007). Whose risk in Philadelphia? Proximity to unequally hazardous industrial facilities. *Social Sciences Quarterly, 88*(2), 515–534.

Stevenson, H. (2014). Representing green radicalism: The limits of state-based representation in global climate change. *Review of International Studies, 40*(1), 177–201.

Waisbord S. (2008). The institutional challenges of participatory communication in international aid. *Social Identities, 14*(4), 505–522.

4 Interrogating metaphors of sustainability

Laying the framework for a more inclusive discussion of the development of the Alberta oil sands for Indigenous groups

Amanda Williams

Introduction

In the context of environmental communication practices, sustainability is a concept that can be challenging to define. Debates over this term began in the 1970s (Clugston & Calder, 1999), and now involve negotiations as scholars aim to imagine the future of the planet and the resources people need to function in their everyday lives. In their comprehensive review of sustainability, Kates, Parris, and Leiserowitz (2005) remarked that it is often "creatively ambiguous," thus allowing "government, civil society, business, and industry to each project their interests, hopes and aspirations" onto the concept (p. 2). Put differently, people often attach a specific meaning to this word in order to justify certain actions or future plans.

This chapter is motivated by a desire to explore the relevance and power of metaphor for shaping the dialogue about the Alberta oil sands and sustainability. The topic of oil sands has received attention both nationally and internationally due to questionable environmental practices and health concerns linked to water and air quality in surrounding communities where extraction is occurring (Paskey, Steward, & Williams, 2013). It has been recognized that in the last decade additional voices and visions about the oil sands have emerged, which was generated largely by one event: the drowning of 1,600 ducks in one of Syncrude's tailings ponds in April 2008 (Paskey et al., 2013; Nelson, Krogman, Johnston, & St. Clair, 2015). Moreover, it has been noted that in the last decade that industry has made a concrete effort to include discussions about oil sands in the context of a wider sustainability lens. In fact, industry players have replaced the idea of corporate social responsibility with a more holistic social, economic, and environmental focus (Paskey et al., 2013). Consequently, understanding what these different dimensions of sustainability have come to mean becomes all the more relevant. This chapter investigates several research questions. How are the mass media and other stakeholder communities (business, not for profit, and government) defining sustainability? Second, how are these groups understanding and experiencing the Alberta oil sands via different sustainability metaphors? Finally, what specific presences and absences about sustainability may offer promise for a more inclusive dialogue with Indigenous groups?

Background: the Alberta oil sands and First Nations communities

Canada has 172 billion barrels of oil that can be recovered economically with today's technology. Of this total, 166 billion barrels are located in the oil sands. Concentrated mainly in the province of Alberta, 80% of these oil sands deposits require in situ technology (i.e., drilling) as opposed to open pit mining (CAPP, 2015, p. 6).

The social issues associated with the development of the oil sands are complex and often oversimplified (Nelson et al., 2015; Paskey et al., 2013; Tran, 2014; Way, 2011, 2013). Some of the most pressing and immediate concerns include the impact of resource development on Indigenous communities, long-term planning and infrastructure funding for municipalities in the Fort McMurray region, the influence of transient workers on social stability, and the effects of the oil sands on education, to name only a few (Paskey et al., 2013). An important issue about race and the environment is how the interests of First Nations and Métis groups are being negotiated since they are a minority group with a large interest in how this area is managed.

First Nations is a term used to describe Aboriginal peoples in Canada who are not Métis or Inuit. First Nations are those peoples who historically lived in North America, from the Atlantic to the Pacific, below the Arctic. In contrast, the Métis descend from the historical joining of First Nations members and Europeans. Both of these groups have been actively involved in consultative efforts regarding the Alberta oil sands (Government of Alberta, 2007). First Nations are organized into governing units called bands, which the Indian Act of 1876 instituted in Canada. The Métis are not bands under this act, so they are often talked about as communities. Indigenous is a term that is used interchangeably with Aboriginal to be inclusive of both First Nations and Métis (Indigenous Corporate Training Inc., 2016).

A present, the area with the largest number of First Nations impacted by this issue is that of Wood Buffalo. Wood Buffalo is a municipality in northeastern Alberta that was formed in 1995 as a result of partnership between Fort McMurray (the city) and District No. 143. It is one of the largest municipalities in the province and has seen the most rapid growth in population, increasing by 9.2% since 2011 (The Canadian Press, 2017). Its current population is 71,589. Within this overall demographic, the area has a population of about 6,400 First Nation residents, who are members of different bands, including the Mikisew Cree First Nation (MCFN), the Athabasca Chipewyan First Nation (ACFN), the Fort McKay First Nation, the Fort McMurray No. 468 First Nation, and the Chipewyan Prairie Dene First Nation (Government of Canada, 2016). There are also six Métis groups which represent approximately 5,000–6,000 residents (Government of Canada, 2016).

In addition to these specific bands and Métis communities, there are at least 26 other First Nations bands across the province that report they are impacted in the Athabasca, Cold Lake, and Peace River oil sands regions (see the 2007 Government of Alberta's Aboriginal Consultation document for a list of these communities). Each of these groups brings its own view and set of issues to the negotiation table when imagining what the consultation process for extracting this resource should look like. For instance, some bands or communities have expressed excitement about the economic possibilities generated by oil sands development (as expressed in the Peace River Métis Consultation Session); others such as ACFN and MCFN have argued for a halt on new projects until their specific concerns (in relation to water, health, reclamation, etc.) have been addressed. There is also a real difference in those groups that chose to deploy legal discussion around land rights versus those that communicated just a broad concern with the environmental impact of oil sands over the relationship being created with "Mother Earth" (Government of Alberta, 2007).

Alberta has three populated treaty areas covered by Treaty 6 (1876), Treaty 7 (1877), and Treaty 8 (1899). These treaties are legal agreements that were negotiated between the federal government and various First Nations to describe rights, benefits and obligations of both parties. By signing these treaties, Aboriginal peoples gave up large portions of land to the government in exchange for reserve land and the right to hunt, trap, and fish on ancestral land. The Canadian federal, provincial, and territorial governments all have a legal duty to consult with and accommodate First Nations groups if their rights may be impacted by development on or near their reserve land. Many of the oil sands projects in Alberta can be found in just such areas (CAPP, 2015). At present, various First Nations and Métis communities are worried about the cumulative impact that developments have on their water, land, air, and animals because it influences their ability to practice their traditional lifestyle and compromises their health. Some scholars have even gone so far as to suggest that oil sands mega projects perpetuate an "industrial genocide" on these peoples (Huseman & Short,

2012). While First Nations groups have been active participants in the regulatory hearings that grant approval of industry oil sands projects, they are also increasingly voicing their discontent via lawsuits, even going so far as to propose a moratorium on all new development in Alberta for the next five years (Government of Alberta, 2007; Wolhberg, 2013).

There is likely not going to be a halt in oil sands project approval, but there remains a duty to consult with affected communities in order to negotiate their social and environmental concerns. Consequently, one way to understand these goals is to examine the definitions and metaphors that different groups use to define the issue of sustainability and the "interests, hopes and aspirations" (Kates et al., 2005) they attach to this ambiguous term.

Metaphor: what is it and why does it matter?

Metaphor is often considered a play on words and part of a larger category of language tools known as the tropes. Other tropes that are often studied in rhetorical analysis include metonyms, synecdoche, and irony. Nevertheless, metaphor is considered by many to be the most complex and therefore the most appealing figure of speech open to investigation (Tilley, 2002). The Greek roots of the term are meta which means "over" and phereras which means "to carry" (Foss, 2017), thus encapsulating what it has come to represent in more modern terms as "understanding and experiencing one kind of things in terms of another" (Lakoff & Johnson, 1980, p. 5).

Contemporary theories of metaphors, such as the one first advanced by Lakoff and Johnson (1980) in their seminal work *Metaphors We Live By*, offer a sharp contrast to classic views of metaphor which tend to dismiss metaphor as unimportant (Hamilton, 2000; Ortony, 1979). They asserted:

> Most people think we can get along perfectly well without metaphor . . . we have found on the contrary, that metaphor is pervasive in everyday life, not just in language but in thought and action. Our ordinary conceptual system, in terms of which we both think and act, is fundamentally metaphorical in nature.
>
> (p. 3)

As this quotation reveals, Lakoff and Johnson (1980) saw metaphor as an important analytical departure point for those interested in understanding how people communicate.

To Lakoff and Johnson (1980), metaphor is as an essential part of how people communicate and respond to the environment around them. They argued:

> Metaphor is not a harmless exercise in naming. It is one of the principle means by which we understand our experience and reason on the basis

of that understanding. To the extent that we act on our reasoning, metaphor plays a role in the creation of reality.

(p. 79)

They are thus suggesting that metaphors have real material consequences. People not only think in metaphor but also the metaphors they use actually shape their reality. For example, Lakoff and Johnson (1980) suggested that *argument is war* is a key metaphor within our current cultural context. Consequently, people talk about arguments using war-like terminology. This is expressed in statements such as "your claims are indefensible," "I won the argument," and "he shot down all that I said" (pp. 4–6). Moreover, individuals also act as though arguments are battles, though they are not in actual combat, by treating the people they are arguing with as opponents and by structuring their argument to try to achieve victory (Lakoff & Johnson, 1980).

Another key dimension that contemporary theories of metaphor have highlighted is that metaphors always mask or hide specific components of how people interact. As Lakoff and Johnson (1980) noted, metaphorical structuring is always partial and never total: "if it were total one concept would be the other, not merely be understood in terms of it" (p. 13). Or as Burke (1966) stated, no matter how much individuals believe they are representing reality, they are only ever able to offer a selection of a reality. With each metaphorical exchange, people are involved in the process of directing intentions in a particular manner. For example, individuals could choose to construct argument not as war but rather as dance (Lakoff & Johnson, 1980).

Finally, Lakoff and Johnson (1980) asserted that metaphors have the ability to become such a natural part of our conversation, so self-evident, that we often forget that alternative metaphors and language is available. Moreover, as Black (1993) noted, metaphors have the potential to self-certify by generating the very reality to which they seem to draw attention. Metaphor is not implicitly a direct misrepresentation or manipulation of the social world, but rather "a mode of representation that can be used, abused and contested" (Tilley, 1999, p. 10). Thus, looking at use and points of contention make metaphor a useful site for appreciating of some of the culturally bounded rationalities that can either encourage or discourage inclusion in regard to the Alberta oil sands.

The Alberta oil sands, sustainability, First Nations, and metaphor

A general search within Google Scholar of the Alberta oil sands and sustainability in the past five years generates predominantly technical articles about how to increase efficiencies via new extraction possibilities, carbon storage and capture, or remediation. Investigations about monitoring water, wild-life, and air quality are also available (see for example Borkenhagen & Cooper, 2016; Dayyani, Daly, & Vandenberg, 2016; Verbeke, Osiyevskyy, & Backman, 2017). While such contributions are significant for advancing the scientific dialogue about this topic, few studies grounded in the social sciences and humanities that have focused on the intersection of these two interests (sustainability and the oil sands) exist. Moreover, when searching sustainability and oil sands and First Nations, fewer articles appear and their focus tends to be on health broadly and/or on air, water, or food contamination (such as Bari & Kindzierski, 2015; Davidson & Spink, 2017; Martin, 2015).

Some notable exceptions to these more scientific studies include Paskey et al. (2013) who investigated the changing nature of oil sands discourses over the past 40 years in regard to broad social, economic, and environmental themes, noting some distinct shifts in language deployment, voices heard, and quality of dialogue. In addition, Berry's (2015) examined industry views of oil sands and noted that metaphors of sustainability as a person and sustainability as a journey are prevalent. Moreover, Sutton's (2017) look at various stakeholders concluded that the language they chose tends to be vague and focused more on practices and values, with goals and indicators figuring much less prominently. Such studies provide a useful departure point upon which this chapter builds.

In terms of First Nations and the oil sands, some interesting observations have been drawn. For example, Parsons and Ray (2016) argued convincingly that by branding the oil sands in Alberta as "ethical oil" and labeling production companies as "sustainable," public and private sectors appear to offer an essential public service while misdirecting attention away from acts of colonialism that make such resources available. Spink and Abel (2015) also recommended a shift in governments' and regulators' mindset to one in which they are meaningfully "working with" Indigenous groups as opposed to simply "dealing with" such communities. Despite the possibility for misdirection on how consultation is presented and thought about, Wanvik and Caine (2017) have noted that rather than being simply subject to circumstance (and just victims of exploitation), Indigenous communities can, and often do, seize appropriate moments of mobilization through strategic and pragmatic engagement.

Explorations of media constructions of the Alberta oil sands are also becoming more common. For example, Way (2013) looked at coverage of oil sands issues in six English-Canadian newspapers from 2005 to 2007. She detected a strongly neo-liberal agenda that absolved industry blame and discredited many of the policy instruments that government could deploy to address sector challenges. Moreover, Tran (2014) explored news coverage from 2007 to 2009 in five Canadian newspapers. The coverage focused on the positive economic aspects of the oil sands, with less attention given to the ecological, political, scientific, and other dimensions of this industry. Additionally, Gunster and Saurette (2014) examined the principal storylines within a major daily newspaper from 2010 to 2011. They concluded that the core narrative was one that defended industry and dismissed environmental criticism of the oil sands; it also promoted the idea that the provincial government must aim to be a "petro-state" that actively champions industry interests. Finally, Nelson et al. (2015) analyzed newspaper coverage of the 1,600 ducks that drowned in a tailings pond in April 2008. They uncovered that most solutions to the issue were short-term and tended to pit economic priorities against environmental concerns in the context of energy development. They also remarked on the lack of Aboriginal sources used to comment on this issue, concluding that the views of local residents, employees, and other members of the public who are most impacted by the environmental effects of industry are rarely heard. This marginalization of certain voices is a finding that also appeared in Paskey et al. (2013).

Broader discussions of sustainability metaphors are becoming increasingly available as well, highlighting the power of language to define the context of debates for key stakeholders. For example, Larson (2011) suggests there is a great deal of urgency in examining the social context of the environmental metaphors (for example, the Earth as a goddess metaphor versus the Earth as a machine metaphor). Moreover, Milne, Kearins, and Walton (2006) have looked at the problematic nature of the sustainability as journey metaphor in business dialogues since it rarely articulates the destination of industry thus often promoting a "business as usual" approach to respecting the environment. Studies such as these provide important context for conceptualizing a wider discursive space for the understanding of this resource and a broader discussion of what it means to talk about sustainability.

In sum, existing literature on the oil sands, sustainability, and First Nations indicate a typically pro-industry stance, a dominant economic frame, and a lack of holistic coverage of the topic particularly regarding impacted communities. Such findings encourage more work in the area, especially investigations that not only focus on one specific stakeholder group (e.g., only the industry or media perspective) to widen the scope and transferability of the results. Some key questions that emerge from this review and inform this analysis are: how widespread is the lack of minority voices in official sustainability reports? Do metaphors like those of the journey and person spread across a wider corpus of stakeholders? How well developed are the metaphors that are commonly deployed by stakeholders? Are there discursive spaces for strategic and pragmatic engagement for Indigenous groups in certain metaphors?

Method

Data sources and sample

Whereas prior research has tended to examine the oil sands more broadly, without a sustainability lens, and often focused on one stakeholder community (either the media or industry), this chapter is looking at a broader set of documentation in various communities. A corpus of sustainability documents from the different communities of interest was compiled for this project. Document compilation involved a search of the Cumulative Environmental Management Association's (CEMA) technical database on the oil sands and also the websites of major oil companies and non-governmental organizations (NGOs) that have an interest in oil sands. In addition, the CBCA Complete and Canada Newstand were used to generate the media sample. Search terms included "oil sands," "oilsands," "tar sands" or "tarsands," "sustainab*," "sustainable development," and "environment*." An effort was also made to look at the websites of impacted First Nations bands and Métis communities to seek any official documents on this subject.

This search resulted in 159 documents, including 16 from government sources, 25 from industry sources, 32 from NGOs, and 86 news documents. A keyword search for "sustain" in each of the documents was then conducted, and 734 excerpts were isolated. An excerpt in this case refers to a complete idea about sustainability.

Analytic method

Metaphor in this instance draws upon the cognitive linguistic tradition and can be defined as "understanding and experiencing one kind of thing in terms of another" (Lakoff & Johnson, 1980, p. 5). The significance of using Lakoff and Johnson's work means that metaphor is understood as consisting of three parts: the source domain, which is often a concrete object, basic schemata, or a semi-concrete entity based on a sensory or bodily experience; the target domain, an abstract concept not easily expressed in literal terms; and the mappings, or the bridge in between the target and source domains, which permits individuals to cognitively appreciate the juxtaposition of the two domains (Kövecses, 2006). In their analytical approach, Lakoff and Johnson (1980) defined as the "conceptual metaphor" the general structure in which the mappings occur and suggested that accompanying linguistic words or phrases be described as "metaphorical linguistic expressions." Thus, in the example *love is a journey*, the target domain is "love" and the source domain is "journey." The conceptual correspondences, or mappings, between the source and target domains include the travelers as the lovers, the vehicle as the love relationship, the destination as the purpose of the relationship, the distance covered as the progress made in the relationship, and obstacles along the way as the difficulties encountered in the relationship. Put another way, these conceptual mappings all contribute to making *love as a journey* a concept that people can understand (Kövecses, 2006).

This current examination of sustainability involved positioning sustainability as the target of the metaphor to be understood in relation to concrete sources following the protocol provided by Lakoff and Johnson (1980) and used by others (Foss, 2017; Williams, 2010). After identifying the occurrences of metaphorical linguistic expressions, the utterances were grouped together, and possible conceptual metaphors were identified. The word "possible" is used to acknowledge that the selection of these categories is the choice of the analyst and thus subjective but can be justified with the presentation of specific excerpts in use (Schmitt, 2005).

Key findings

Several key findings emerged. First, it was rare to encounter articulations of the First Nations and Métis position. About one-third of the corpus had a mention of First Nations and Métis groups (52 documents). Companies like Nexen, Shell, Suncor, Statoil, Syncrude, and the Oil Sand Leadership Initiative, all highlighted Aboriginal programs. However, they mostly speak on behalf of what they do for these communities and very rarely included their specific voices (via direct quote or specific positions about sustainability). Media accounts tended sometimes to use a First Nations person as a source but were just as likely to quote a lawyer or government official about sustainability issues in relation to these groups. This finding may help explain why some Indigenous groups are in fact wanting to see the stop of the development of any new projects (Government of Alberta, 2007; Wolhberg, 2013): why would people want to support a process that fails to represent them in a meaningful way? Moreover, while metaphor has been shown to be an effective tool based on what it includes or excludes (Tilley, 1999), the power of metaphor also seems to remain in the hands of those who actually have the resources to talk about sustainability versus those who do not. In the context of the Alberta oil sands, this corpus suggests that Indigenous groups are rarely the primary authors of their own stories about sustainability and by extension had very little space to invoke metaphors that had meaning to them.

A second finding of note is that there tended to be very few complete definitions of sustainability in reports about the oil sands. Vague references to the concepts of sustainability were common. Typical ways to describe sustainability were as an economic, environmental, social, or community process. While linkages among such processes provide a general frame for situating the concept of sustainability, when read in the context of the documents as a whole it was apparent that little else was specified about these dimensions. For example, what does it mean to be socially sustainable and/ or create sustainable communities? Or how does environmental sustainability differ from economic sustainability? Moreover, how these dimensions might be measured or estimated was rarely presented. The corpus demonstrated that broad sources tended to be attached to sustainability as a target. Illustrations of this were references to sustainability as a "project," "system," "mindset," "way of living," or "concept," with no other details. This made analyzing the concept of sustainability more challenging since it was rarely elaborated upon. In addition, oftentimes quite technical language was used that gave little formal guidance to the reader about how to better appreciate the dimensions of sustainability provided. The excerpt below taken from an NGO report is a typical example of this generality in practice:

> Sustainable development can be defined as development that generates horizontal or downward sloping cumulative impact curves below threshold levels for important management indicators.
>
> (NGO: Kennett & Schneider, 2008)

This excerpt deploys the *sustainability as a metric* metaphor linked to economics, with no discussion in the immediate context of what important management indicators were being referred to.

A third finding of note, the most commonly deployed metaphors tended to be focused on the idea of using an accounting framework known as the "triple bottom line" (Slaper & Hall, 2011) to conceptualize sustainability, and metaphors involving movement. For example, quite often in discussions across all the discourse communities was a view of sustainability that balanced economic, environmental, and social/political dimensions. Sometimes the metaphor of balance was used (e.g., how to weigh decisions that impact sustainability), but more often all three factors appeared in discussions, implying a desire to reach symmetry. This attempt to manage potentially conflicting priorities takes the form most distinctly in the use of "triple bottom line" language. Some illustrations of this articulation in practice included the following excerpts:

> Suncor pursues a "triple bottom line vision" of sustainable development – we maintain that energy development should occur in a way that provides economic prosperity, promotes social well-being and preserves a healthy environment.
>
> (Industry: Suncor, 2012)

The program will focus on the triple bottom line of sustainability performance – economic, social and environmental.

(Industry: OSLI, 2012)

Views of sustainability as either a journey or, more generally, movement were also common across all discourse communities. This included the explicit use of the journey language as it relates to both oils sands development and company culture. It also involved broad references to stepping, running, and keeping pace. There were also mentions of charting the course and designing road maps. Specific examples of this metaphor in the data included:

While we won't always agree, I believe our differences can be overcome. In the most fundamental way, we are on this sustainability journey together. Let's keep our eye on the road and reach our destination safely and responsibly.

(Industry: Suncor, 2014)

Optimists hope it is a small step toward sustainability at a time when the federal government is backing away from green energy.

(Media: Riley, 2012)

In a speech in Vancouver Wednesday, Mr. Balsillie, now chairman of Sustainable Development Technology Canada (SDTC), said framing the debate as "for or against the oil sands" is unproductive and will "keep us from moving forward in a meaningful way." It's innovation that will "truly put ourselves on a path towards sustainability," he said.

(Media: Catteno, 2014)

The idea of journey and movement is captured in the ideas of keeping one's eye on the road, taking steps toward sustainability, and the perception that there is a specific path to being sustainable that can be followed.

Yet, there was some indication that the mass media and NGO communities realize that current articulations of sustainability are not helpful in promoting a meaningful or fulsome discussion view about this resource as the following quotes demonstrate:

Industry welcomes new ideas to "improve our performance," but seems to be like so many for whom "sustainability" means being able to carry on doing whatever they're doing without interference from government, environmental activists, aging rockers or, probably, aged columnists.

(Media: Hunter, 2014)

Economic, social and ecological objectives are promoted under the banner of sustainability in the absence of careful analysis of the preconditions for achieving these objectives or the relationships among them.

(NGO: Kennett & Schneider, 2008)

Both critiques are critical of the *sustainability as metric* metaphor. They highlight the fact that this concept, while often deployed, is rarely unpacked and questioned. This specific observation challenges the existing scholarship about how the media cover the oil sands, which has tended to present stories on this topic that do not criticize the status quo (such as Gunster & Saurette, 2014; Way, 2013), though it is worth noting the aforementioned critiques are few and far between in the excerpts analyzed. Other examples of a more critical stance toward how sustainability is imagined include references to unsustainability. For example, an article on overall growth within society (as it relates to oil and otherwise) stated:

No system can grow forever – neither human nor economic. Yet the pursuit of continuous growth has been the bedrock economic model of our time. Outdated and unsustainable, it is still advocated, recklessly and relentlessly, by federal, provincial and nearly all municipal governments.

(Media: Beaty, 2013)

In this quote *sustainability as a system* is questioned and how long we can sustain a lifestyle that depends on oil is alluded to. Another example comes from activist David Suzuki, who asks:

Do we gain comfort and happiness by driving inefficient automobiles, buying and scrapping and then buying more stuff that we must work harder to pay for, and selling resources to enrich the fossil fuel industry and to allow other countries to follow our unsustainable path?

(Media: Suzuki, 2012)

Here the idea of *sustainability as a journey* is being interrogated since Suzuki is asking whether the "path" chosen by countries to develop using a specific type of energy is indeed the best route available. A final illustration of this more critical stance deals directly with First Nations concerns:

The Treaty 8 First Nations of Alberta stated that resource developments in Northern Alberta are "proceeding at an unsustainable pace that threatens the environment which First Nations people rely upon to pursue their constitutionally protected Treaty Rights.

(NGO: Grant, Dagg, Dyer, & Lemphers, 2010)

This excerpt critiques the *sustainability as movement* metaphor by talking about a pace which from a literal sense is the maintenance of consistent and continuous speed when moving. In doing so the reader is reminded that the way resources are being developed (the movement forward and the speed chosen) does not have a positive impact for First Nations. As these various examples demonstrate, at times mass media and NGO stakeholders were willing to question people's current lifestyles and how they relate to the oil sands, as well as how sustainability is being defined.

Discussion and conclusion

This research began with two research questions. The first was: how are the mass media and other stakeholder communities (business, not for profit, and government) understanding and experiencing the Alberta oil sands via different sustainability metaphors? In response to this query, the current analysis showed that the metaphors being deployed are multifaceted and diverse. Metaphor use can and does vary across discourse communities. For example, the NGO and mass media communities were shown to be critical, at times, of inadequate definitions of sustainability, and even highlighted unsustainable practices. The media as a source of critique of industry practices was not commonly found in previous studies of oil sands coverage (such as Gunster & Saurette, 2014; Way, 2013). Moreover, many of the common metaphors found in the corpus such as *sustainability as a triple bottom line* and *sustainability as a journey* have been observed in other contexts (Audebrand, 2010; Camino, 2014; Clugston & Calder, 1999; Jabareen, 2004; Ihlen & Roper, 2011; Livesey, 2002; Milne et al., 2006). It also became apparent in this investigation that defining sustainability is still an area where many of the metaphors being deployed remain vague and difficult to articulate. This is not an uncommon finding, and has been reported in previous studies of metaphor as well (see for example Haase, 2013).

Put another way, this investigation shows that the creative ambiguity that Kates et al. (2005) saw in the literature on sustainability over a decade ago is still clearly present in a study of the oil sands and sustainability. Whether this ambiguity is strategic or purposeful (Eisenberg, 1984; Leitch & Davenport, 2007), or present simply because consistent narratives are still being actively negotiated, as is the case with climate change (DiFrancesco & Young, 2011), is difficult to determine. It is also possible in regard to the Alberta oil sands and sustainability that this ambiguity will always be necessary in order to unite participants with seemingly incommensurable positions (Leitch & Davenport, 2007). The goal in this case is thus not to find the best metaphor for sustainability and the Alberta oil sands but rather to question those being used and consider how they can be deployed more effectively to promote metaphorical pluralism (Audebrand, 2010) or meta-phorical multiplicity (Carew & Mitchell, 2006).

The second research question this investigation set out to determine was: what specific presences and absences offer the most promise for expanding a dialogue with Indigenous groups and other marginalized communities? Starting with absences, it is worth noting that it has been recognized in the existing literature that when it comes to sustainability, Aboriginal environmental perspectives (and Indigenous perspectives more broadly) "have largely been ignored or trivialized" (Beckford, Jacobs, Williams, & Nahdee, 2010, p. 240). This can perhaps be explained by the "tensions that exist between traditional cultures and knowledge on the one hand and Western Eurocentric notions of science and scientific knowing on the other vis-a-vis their legitimacy" (Beckford et al., 2010, p. 240). This paper supports this finding in two ways. First, in the collection of documents for analysis it was apparent how rare it was to encounter the First Nations and Métis position at all. Moreover, when documents did mention concerns, Indigenous groups were rarely the primary authors of their own stories. Secondly, many of the metaphors in the documents analyzed focused on the highly technical and economic dimensions of the oil sands with very few references to traditional knowledge assessments. There was, however, an occasional reference in the corpus to developing a sustainability mindset, which is perhaps a little closer to a more culturally embedded and situated view. Clearly, the next step for research in this area is to look at what metaphors seem to have uptake in these communities. Ethnographic work seems advisable in this case because as many have noted, First Nations knowledge is often oral and symbolic, passed on via modeling, practicing, and animation as opposed to via the written word (Battiste, 2002; Beckford et al., 2010). We can also ask: is open and unconstrained dialogue possible when it comes to the oil sands and sustainability? Moreover, if it is not possible, what responses are appropriate? Such questions have been posed within the healthcare field (Gillespie, Reader, Cornish, & Campbell, 2014) but are also highly appropriate to a politically sensitive issue like the oil sands.

Despite these absences, it can also be argued that some rich dialogues using many of the metaphors already in circulation might be possible. These metaphors could be extended and perhaps in doing so encourage the kind of pragmatic engagement that was noted as possible by Wanvik and Caine (2017) and potentially foster the mindset change recommended by Spink and Abel (2015). For example, while metaphors such as *sustainability as balance/triple bottom line* and *sustainability as a journey* have tended to simplify the complexity of oil sands development because they have not been fully developed, they both still raise important questions about how this resource ought to be handled. An illustration of what a next level of interrogation could look like, in terms of probes associated with a particular metaphor, can be found in the following.

Sustainability as balance/triple bottom line

Those who approach the idea of the triple bottom line more critically have noted that the challenge with the metaphor is not in defining what is meant by it but rather in developing key ways to measure it, find appropriate data, and present final numbers around what are acceptable trade-offs (Slaper & Hall, 2011). This metaphor raises some questions: can empirical measures of oil sands' environmental and social impact be easily captured and value ascertained? Can the social pressures being placed on a community like Fort McMurray be economically quantified for integration with the financial profit and loss statement? Is the weighting equal? What do First Nations and Métis groups think of this metaphor? Does it resonate with them? Could industry be more explicit about the sorts of metrics they use to measure their activities and to judge the performance of industry? For example, in the case of oil sands and sustainable development there are a few different frameworks that can be drawn upon: (1) the Oil and Gas Industry Voluntary Guidance on Sustainability Reporting from IPIECA (an oil and gas industry association whose name is no longer an abbreviation), the American Petroleum Institute, and the International Association of Oil and Gas Producers; (2) the United Nations Global Compact, an initiative for businesses to align their operations and strategies with broad sustainable development goals; and (3) the Global Reporting Initiative, whose guidelines offer a comprehensive set of indicators covering all dimensions of sustainable development.

Sustainability as a journey

The journey metaphor can be a misleading one as it can cause one to forget that sustainability is an ongoing process and not something that has already been achieved. This metaphor raises some core questions: what is the start and end point to this journey? How do we know when we have arrived? What are potential side trips, roadblocks, and detours? Who is invited along for the ride and who is being left behind? And most importantly, what would it take to make First Nations and Métis more visible travelers on this journey?

To conclude, metaphors of sustainability for the Alberta oil sands need a much clearer conceptualization if they are to help promote a constructive dialogue about this resource. Useful building blocks for supporting deep and engaged conversations are already there but need to be probed and interrogated more fully to be truly helpful. In addition, more work has to also be done with First Nations and Métis in Alberta, in order to see what metaphorical conceptualizations they chose to invoke when trying to understand and experience the impact of the oil sands within their communities. The ultimate goal in this case would be to compile "Aboriginal examples, illustrations, evidence, analogies, and cases to elucidate ecological concepts and issues" (Beckford et al., 2010, p. 247). Doing so could open up many new avenues of learning that have been previously overlooked and make what is at present a very shallow understanding of industry activity a more robust conversation about the costs and benefits the oil sands generate that more effectively stretches across racial lines and is inclusive of all voices instead of predominantly those who are already powerful.

References

Audebrand, L. (2010). Sustainability in strategic management education: The quest for new root metaphors. *Academy of Management Learning & Education, 9*(3), 413–428. doi:10.5465/AMLE.2010.53791824

Bari, M., & Kindzierski, W. B. (2015). Fifteen-year trends in criteria air pollutants in oil sands communities of Alberta, Canada. *Environment International, 74*, 200–208.

Battiste, M. (2002). *Indigenous knowledge and pedagogy in First Nations education: A literature review with recommendations*. Ottawa: Apamuwek Institute.

Beaty, R. (2013). Forget growth. *The Vancouver Sun*, A11.

Beckford, C. L., Jacobs, C., Williams, N., & Nahdee, R. (2010). Aboriginal environmental wisdom, stewardship, and sustainability: Lessons from the Walpole Island First Nations, Ontario, Canada. *The Journal of Environmental Education, 41*(4), 239–248.

Berry, M. N. (2015). Sustainability As: An analysis of the Alberta oil sands industry's metaphorical discourse. *Consilience: The Journal of Sustainable Development, 14*(2), 46–70.

Black, M. (1993). More about metaphor. In A. Ortony (Ed.), *Metaphor and thought* (pp. 19–41). New York, NY: Cambridge University Press.

Borkenhagen, A., & Cooper, D. J. (2016). Creating fen initiation conditions: A new approach for peatland reclamation in the oil sands region of Alberta. *Journal of Applied Ecology, 53*(2), 550–558.

Burke, K. (1966). *Language as symbolic action*. Los Angeles, CA: University of California Press.

CAPP. (2015). *The facts on the oilsands*. Retrieved from www.oscaalberta.ca/wp-content/uploads/2015/08/The-Facts-on-Oil-Sands-2015.pdf

Camino, E. (2014). How to devise a sustainable science for sustainability? A reflexive approach for the present time. *E3S Web of Conferences, 2*(04001), 1–5. doi:10.1051/e3sconf/20140204001

The Canadian Press. (2017). New census data: Population of wood buffalo outpaced national growth rate. *Metro News*. Retrieved from www.metronews.ca/news/

canada/2017/02/08/new-census-data-population-of-wood-buffalo-outpaced-national-growth-rate.html

Carew, A. L., & Mitchell, C. A. (2006). Metaphors used by some engineering academics in Australia for understanding and explaining sustainability. *Environmental Education Research, 12*(2), 217–231.

Catteno, C. (2014, March 27). Clean-tech clash over oil sands; Balsille, Steyer at odds on sustainability. *The National Post*, FP3.

Clugston, R. M., & Calder, W. (1999). Critical dimensions of sustainability in higher education. *Sustainability and University Life, 5*, 31–46.

Davidson, C., & Spink, D. (2017). Alternate approaches for assessing impacts of oil sands development on air quality: A case study using the First Nation Community of Fort McKay. *Journal of the Air & Waste Management Association, 68*(4), 308–328.

Dayyani, S., Daly, G., & Vandenberg, J. (2016). Approach to assessing the effects of aerial deposition on water quality in the Alberta oil sands region. *Water Environment Research, 88*(2), 175–189.

DiFrancesco, D. A., & Young, N. (2011). Seeing climate change: The visual construction of global warming in Canadian national print media. *Cultural Geographies, 18*(4), 517–536.

Eisenberg, E. M. (1984). Ambiguity as strategy in organizational communication. *Communication Monographs, 51*(3), 227–242.

Foss, S. (2017). *Rhetorical criticism: Exploration and practice* (5th ed.). Long Grove, IL: Waveland Press Inc.

Gillespie, A., Reader, T., Cornish, F., & Campbell, C. (2014). Beyond ideal speech situations: Adapting to communication asymmetries in health care. *Journal of Health Psychology, 19*(1), 72–78.

Government of Alberta. (2007). *Oil Sands consultations: Aboriginal consultation final report*. Retrieved from https://open.alberta.ca/publications/3952776

Government of Canada. (2016). *Oil sands: A strategic resource for Canada, North America and the global market*. Retrieved from www.nrcan.gc.ca/sites/www.nrcan.gc.ca/files/energy/pdf/oilsands-sablesbitumineux/14-0696%20Oil%20Sands%20-%20Indigenous%20Peoples_e.pdf

Grant, J., Dagg, J., Dyer, S., & Lemphers, N. (2010). *Northern lifeblood: Empowering northern leaders to protect the Mackenzie River Basin from oil sands risks*. Drayton Valley, Alberta, Canada: The Pembina Institute.

Gunster, S., & Saurette, P. (2014). Storylines in the sands: News, narrative, and ideology in the Calgary Herald. *Canadian Journal of Communication, 39*(3), 333.

Haase, S. (2013). An engineering dilemma: Sustainability in the eyes of future technology professionals. *Science and Engineering Ethics, 19*(3), 893–911. doi:10.1007/s11948-012-9417-0

Hamilton, A. (2000). Metaphor in theory and practice: The influence of metaphor on expectations. *ACM Journal of Computer Documentation, 24*(4), 237–253.

Hunter, I. (2014, January 19). Industry chiefs dislike 'off-oil' remarks. *Times Colonist*.

Huseman, J., & Short, D. (2012). 'A slow industrial genocide': Tar sands and the Indigenous peoples of northern Alberta. *The International Journal of Human Rights, 16*(1), 216–237.

Ihlen, Ø., & Roper, J. (2011). Corporate reports on sustainability and sustainable development: 'We have arrived'. *Sustainable Development, 22*(1), 42–51. doi:10.1002/2d.524

Indigenous Corporate Training Inc. (2016). *Indigenous peoples terminology guidelines for usage*. Blog post. Retrieved from www.ictinc.ca/blog/indigenous-peoples-terminology-guidelines-for-usage

Jabareen, Y. (2004). A knowledge map for describing variegated and conflict domains of sustainable development. *Journal of Environmental Planning and Management, 47*(4), 623–642. doi:10.1080/0964056042000243267

Kates, R. W., Parris, T. M., & Leiserowitz, A. A. (2005). What is sustainable development? *Environment, 47*(3), 8.

Kennett, S. A., & Schneider, R. R. (2008). *Making it real: Implementing Alberta's land-use framework*. Pembina Institute for Appropriate Development. Retrieved from http://www.pembina.org/pub/1715

Kövecses, Z. (2006). *Language, mind, and culture: A practical introduction*. Oxford: Oxford University Press.

Lakoff, G., & Johnson, M. (1980). *Metaphors we live by*. Chicago, IL: The University of Chicago Press.

Larson, B. (2011). *Metaphors for environmental sustainability: Redefining our relationship with nature*. New Haven, CT: Yale University Press.

Leitch, S., & Davenport, S. (2007). Strategic ambiguity as a discourse practice: The role of keywords in the discourse on 'sustainable' biotechnology. *Discourse Studies, 9*(1), 43–61.

Livesey, S. M. (2002). The discourse of the middle ground: Citizen Shell commits to sustainable development. *Management Communication Quarterly, 15*(3), 313–349. doi:10.1177/0893318902153001

Martin, J. W. (2015). The challenge: Safe release and reintegration of oil sands process-affected water. *Environmental Toxicology and Chemistry, 34*(12), 2682–2682.

Milne, M. J., Kearins, K., & Walton, S. (2006). Creating adventures in wonderland: The journey metaphor and environmental sustainability. *Organization, 13*(6), 801–839. Chicago.

Nelson, P., Krogman, N., Johnston, L., & St. Clair, C. C. (2015). Dead ducks and dirty oil: Media representations and environmental solutions. *Society & Natural Resources, 28*(4), 345–359.

Ortony, A. (1979). *Metaphor and thought*. Cambridge: Cambridge University Press.

OSLI. (2012). *The collaborative way: Oil sands leadership initiative*. Retrieved from www.sciconnect.ca/uploads/files/OSLI_Collaborative_Report_2012.pdf

Parsons, S., & Ray, E. (2016). Sustainable colonization: Tar sands as resource colonialism. *Capitalism Nature Socialism*, 1–19.

Paskey, J., Steward, G., & Williams, A. (2013). *The Alberta oil sands then and now: An investigation of the economic, environmental and social discourses across four decades*. OSRIN Report No. TR-38. 108 pp. Retrieved from http://hdl.handle.net/10402/era.32845

Riley, S. (2012, April 27). Redford: A breath of clean air? *The Ottawa Citizen*, A11.

Schmitt, R. (2005). Systematic metaphor analysis as a method of qualitative research. *The Qualitative Report, 10*(2), 358–394.

Slaper, T., & Hall, T. J. (2011). The triple bottom line: What is it and how does it work? *Indiana Business Review*, *86*(1), 4.

Spink, D.R., & Abel, R.C. (2015). Development of Alberta's oil sands: The Fort McKay First Nation's perspective on environmental management. In M. De Bree and H. Ruessink (Eds.), *Innovating environmental compliance assurance* (pp. 227–253). Rotterdam, The Netherlands: International Network for Environmental Compliance and Enforcement.

Suncor (2012). *Report on sustainability*. Retrieved from http://sustainability.suncor.com/2010/default.aspx

Suncor (2014). *Report on sustainability*. Retrieved from http://suncor360.nonfiction.ca/2014/ros-en/

Sutton, M. (2017). Discourses of the Alberta oil sands: What key stakeholders really think about sustainability. *Consilience*, *18*, 175–192.

Suzuki, D. (2012, October 12). Energy plan must be about more than just energy. *Trail Times*, p. 7.

Tilley, C. (1999). *Metaphor and material culture*. Oxford: Blackwell Publishers.

Tilley, C. (2002). Metaphor, materiality and intrepretation. In V. Buchli (Ed.), *The Material Culture Reader* (pp. 23–56). Oxford: Berg.

Tran, L. S. (2014). *Environmental journalism: A case study of the Canadian bituminous sands*. Doctoral dissertation, Concordia University, Canada.

Verbeke, A., Osiyevskyy, O., & Backman, C. A. (2017). Strategic responses to imposed innovation projects: The case of carbon capture and storage in the Alberta oil sands industry. *Long Range Planning*, *50*(5), 684–698.

Wanvik, T. I., & Caine, K. (2017). Understanding Indigenous strategic pragmatism: Métis engagement with extractive industry developments in the Canadian North. *The Extractive Industries and Society*, *4*(3), 595–605.

Way, L. A. (2011). An energy superpower or a super sales pitch? Building the case through an examination of Canadian newspapers coverage of oil sands. *Canadian Political Science Review*, *5*(1), 74–98.

Way, L. A. (2013). *Canadian newspaper coverage of the Alberta oil sands: The intractability of neoliberalism*. Doctoral dissertation, University of Alberta, Canada.

Williams, A. M. (2010). *Metaphor, technology and policy: An investigation of the Alberta SuperNet*. Doctoral thesis, University of Calgary, Canada.

Wolhberg, M. (2013). Chief calls for five-year moratorium on oilsands. *Northern Journal*. Retrieved from https://norj.ca/2013/08/chief-calls-for-five-year-moratorium-on-oilsands/

5 "So that the environment looks clean"

Cultural values and environmental communication in a Nicaraguan community

Jessica Love-Nichols

Introduction

Incomplete solid-waste management is one of the most severe environmental problems faced by Nicaraguan communities (Ardoin & Sivek, 2002; Nading & Fisher, 2017). Discarded trash lines roadways and collects in arroyos, contaminating soil and water and providing a breeding ground for disease-carrying mosquitoes. Of the over 3,000 tons of solid waste generated in the country per day, 34% is transported to dumps and 28% open-air landfills (Hoornweg & Bhada-Tata, 2012, p. 87). The percentages of managed solid waste are higher in major cities, such as Managua, which is reported to cover 80% of generated solid waste (2015, p. 76), and lower in rural areas, although no exact number is given. In the communities that are the focus of this chapter, for instance, there is no centralized waste management system, and all generated trash is managed at the individual level, through incineration, recycling, or dumping in watercourses or other public areas. Contributing to the issue of solid waste mismanagement is a lack of financial resources and institutional infrastructure, but also a lack of cultural consensus surrounding the correct individual behaviors for handling solid waste. In the early 2010s travelers on local busses, for instance, were as likely to see signs above the windows instructing them *tire la basura por la ventana* ("throw trash through the window") as *no tire la basura por la ventana* ("do not throw trash through the window"). Because of the severity of the issue, waste management has also been the focus of many international environmental education campaigns, with organizations such as the Peace Corps, the Rainbow Network, and El Porvenir all devoting a substantial part of their environmental education programs to changing the individual behaviors relating to trash disposal. Furthermore, in 2013 the national government launched a widespread environmental education campaign, in part to promote anti-littering behavior. This moment of dialogue and contestation has foregrounded the environmental values and behaviors surrounding trash disposal in Nicaraguan discourse and perception, providing a unique opportunity for researchers of environmental communication to observe the interaction of these values and pro-environmental behaviors at the local level.

Much work in the environmental social sciences has shown that environmental values are important predictors of pro-environmental behaviors (Corraliza & Berenguer, 2000; Dietz, Fitzgerald, & Shwom, 2005; Hards, 2011; Satterfield, 2001; Schultz & Zelezny, 1998) and an important lens through which environmental messages can be framed (Lakoff, 2010; Miller, 2000). Scholars have furthermore investigated many of the environmental values common in the United States and Europe (Kempton, Boster, & Hartley, 1996), as well as their interaction with values and cultural affiliations not directly pertaining to environmentalism (Coupland & Coupland, 1997; Gromet, Kunreuther, & Larrick, 2013). While researchers have begun to examine how these values may differ across cultures, ethnoracial groups, or linguistic communities (Deng, Walker, & Swinnerton, 2006; Leung & Rice, 2002; Schultz, Unipan, & Gamba, 2000), less is known about how such cultural differences might affect intercultural environmental communication in practice (Lin, 2012). Furthermore, most studies on environmental values generally take a broad view, primarily concerned with identifying factors that predict a general orientation to pro-environmentalism and how to measure the outcome of interventions on the individual level. This chapter, however, takes a more local approach to the study of values – regarding them not only as broad personal characteristics and orientations, but also as social and interactional stances toward cultural practices and ideologies, arguing that it is important to consider – especially across languages and cultures – values as local phenomena grounded in a particular sociocultural context.

In particular, this chapter examines the role of culturally specific values in environmental communication and behavior in Nicaragua. Nicaragua is a productive site in which to study cultural environmental values; it is understudied, with only one study having investigated Nicaraguan environmental attitudes and values (Schultz & Zelezny, 1998). Furthermore, as a low-lying tropical country, Nicaragua is especially susceptible to the effects of global and regional changes in temperature and rainfall patterns, and rural, economically disadvantaged Nicaraguans – like many marginalized communities – are particularly vulnerable to the impacts of environmental degradation. Nicaragua is the second poorest country in the western hemisphere by GDP, highly vulnerable to natural disasters (Herrera et al., 2018), and ranks fourth in the Global Long-term Climate Risk Index from 1993 to 2012 (Kreft & Eckstein, 2014). It is thus vital for scholars and practitioners to understand culturally relevant environmental values in Nicaragua in order to engage with this vulnerable and traditionally marginalized community.

Using ethnographic methods, in this chapter I analyze how environmental values are used and illustrated in Nicaragua in three different discursive contexts, as well as how these values interact with individual behaviors. The first context analyzed is an environmental education campaign begun by the Nicaraguan national government in 2013 called the *Estrategia Nacional Para Vivir Limpio, Vivir Sano, Vivir Bonito, Vivir Bien . . .!* ("National Strategy to Live Cleanly, Live Healthily, Live Beautifully, Live Well . . .!"), a nationwide initiative developed primarily to address the issue of solid waste disposal (Nading & Fisher, 2017). Materials, including posters, pamphlets, and bumper stickers featuring the campaign logo, were distributed widely, and schools received corresponding age-appropriate activities to promote the campaign in the classroom. The second context I analyze in this chapter is a visual environmental education message. This illustration, created by local teachers at an elementary school in a small town in the central Nicaraguan department of Matagalpa, consists of a hand drawn picture and a message in permanent marker on the wall of a latrine. The final context I explore in this chapter, which takes place in a neighboring Matagalpan community, is an individual reflection about an NGO-coordinated "community clean-up."

Through the analysis of these contexts, I find that environmental values in Nicaragua exist as one element of a locally relevant value system, where an orientation to protecting the environment is connected to respecting institutions and maintaining good public health. Crucially, this bundle of values differs in several important ways from Western value systems. There is no dichotomization of nature and humanity, for instance, and the orientation to public health is much more closely connected to environmental protection. Furthermore, environmentalism is seen as pro- rather than anti-establishment (Kempton, Boster, and Hartley, 1996). These differences create considerable implications for the intersection of values and pro-environmental behaviors in Nicaragua, especially in the context of cross-cultural environmental communication. This chapter argues that, in order to fully understand environmental values and behaviors in cross-cultural contexts, environmental communication researchers must draw on ethnographic and discourse analytic methodologies, understanding environmental values as situated within locally relevant frameworks of values and identities. It furthermore contends that practitioners must also strive to situate environmental communication within this context of local values.

Environmental values, beliefs, and attitudes

Over time scholars have found environmental values, as well as environmental beliefs and attitudes, to be important factors in shaping people's decisions (Ives & Kendal, 2014) and have developed several approaches to measure fundamental environmental values. Some of these approaches assess factors specific to nature, such as the New Environmental Paradigm scale, which was conceived to measure beliefs about the relationship of human beings to the environment (Dunlap & Van Liere, 1978; Dunlap, Van Liere, Mertig, & Jones, 2000). Another such approach is the Connectedness to Nature Scale (Mayer & Frantz, 2004), which was designed to "tap into an individual's affective, experiential connection to nature" (p. 504). Other approaches in this research area, like the Universal Values Scale (Schwartz, 1977, 1992, 1994), instead measure general value orientations such as "self-transcendence" versus "self-enhancement," or ecocentrism vs. anthropocentrism (Thompson & Barton, 1994) and correlate those with environmental behaviors (Stern & Dietz, 1994; Stern, Dietz, Kalof, & Guagnano, 1995). The Value Belief Norm Theory links these approaches, connecting environmental values with resulting beliefs (such as New Environmental Paradigm (NEP) beliefs), and ultimately norms and behaviors (Stern, Dietz, Abel, Guagnano, & Kalof, 1999).

A growing body of evidence suggests that many of these measures are reliable predictors of pro-environmental behaviors (Dietz et al., 2005), and although most of the analyses have been completed in Western countries, several studies have begun to expand some of these measures to different cultural contexts. A number of studies uphold the usefulness of the NEP internationally, for instance, in Japan (Pierce, Lovrich, Tsurutani, & Abe, 1986), China (Lo, Fryxell, & Wong, 2006), and Korea (Shin, 2001), but other scholars have raised concerns about the validity of the measure in cross-cultural contexts. Some work has found lower levels of internal consistency and less predictive value in the NEP outside of the US and western Europe (Gooch, 1995; Schultz & Zelezny, 1998), while others have questioned the applicability of the dichotomy between the Human Exceptionalism Paradigm (HEP) – the belief that humans are not subject to or governed by natural conditions – and the NEP – the idea that humans are ecologically interdependent within the natural world – in non-Westernized contexts (Chatterjee, 2008; Corral-Verdugo & Armendáriz, 2000). The Universal Values Scale has also had mixed results in international applications (de Groot & Steg, 2007; Schultz & Zelezny, 1998).

Within research on environmentalism specifically on Hispanic or Latin@ populations, some scholars have argued that Hispanics in the United States, as well as South and Central America, have stronger environmental views than non-Hispanics, as measured by the NEP (Noe & Snow, 1990; Schultz et al., 2000), although other researchers have shown the opposite effect (Johnson, Bowker, & Cordell, 2004). Schultz et al. (2000) also found stronger environmental attitudes (as measured by the NEP) among foreign-born

Latin@s living in the United States, and a negative correlation between acculturation and environmental attitudes. They did not, however, find any difference in pro-environmental behaviors based on national origin or level of acculturation. Only one study to date has examined environmental values in Nicaragua specifically. Schultz and Zelezny (1998) conducted a survey with 78 Nicaraguan college students as part of a larger cross-cultural investigation. While they found scores of self-transcendence to be significantly predictive of pro-environmental behaviors among Nicaraguan students, they did not find the same for the NEP. Furthermore, they found some key differences in behaviors considered to be pro-environmental in Nicaragua compared to metrics commonly used in the United States.

While there has been a great deal of research connecting environmental values and beliefs to pro-environmental behaviors, there are still several outstanding questions. One lesser-studied area, for instance, is the interaction of environmental values and observed pro-environmental behaviors. Since most research on environmental values and behaviors examines self-reported accounts of different behaviors through surveys, more research is needed in order to understand how cultural values relate to observed individual behaviors. Additionally, many of the widely used measures of environmental values and beliefs, while differing in some aspects, take environmental values to be characteristics of the individual, seeing them as "concepts or beliefs" that "transcend specific situations" and "guide selection or evaluation of behavior and events" (Schwartz & Bilsky, 1987, p. 551). Thus, limited work has considered the influence of specific cultural systems on environmental values and behaviors, despite the fact that some researchers have shown culture to be an important determinant of attitudes (Price, Walker, & Boschetti, 2014; Schultz, Unipan et al., 2000). Another approach to the study of environmental values views them as community- or societal-level features fundamentally rooted in culture. Anthropologists Kempton et al. (1996), for instance, analyze the cultural models of environmentalism in the US, finding that US Americans generally describe nature through one of four models, the "model of human reliance on a limited world," or the models of nature as "interdependent," "balanced," or "unpredictable." Other scholars taking a cultural lens have shown environmental values to be intrinsically connected with other, non-environmental values, sharing social meaning. Hoelle (2017), for instance, illustrates that for western Brazilian cowboys, valuing a hygienic and hairless body is connected to the valorization of well-tended pastureland. Furthermore, for some Latino environmentalists living in the US, Peña (2005a, 2005b) demonstrates the connection between the value of stewardship of the land and a rejection of US imperialism. Similarly, Carter (2016) shows the importance of environmental justice for Latin@ ideas of environmentalism in California and argues that this orientation is based in Hispanic and indigenous cultural values (Carter, 2016). This chapter takes a similar approach in examining the values and behaviors surrounding environmental protection in rural Nicaragua. I consider environmental values as community-level features – existing in systems of associated values which vary across cultures – and argue that this perspective on environmental values is important in understanding environmental beliefs and behaviors in cross-cultural contexts.

Waste management in Nicaragua

Inadequate waste disposal creates ongoing environmental and health problems for many rural and urban Nicaraguan communities. Scholars have documented some of the issues surrounding solid waste management, especially with regards to the municipal dump of the capital city of Managua, called La Chureca (Nading & Fisher, 2017). Before its enclosure in 2013, La Chureca was the largest open-air dump in Central America, built on the shores of Lake Managua, and was populated by hundreds of people sorting through the waste to find sellable recyclables (Hartmann, 2018). Many other cities throughout Nicaragua also maintain municipal solid waste management programs, though they vary widely in execution and size, with some municipalities providing trash collection but disposing of the waste in open-air collection sites, while others, such as Managua, have sanitary landfill infrastructure for the disposal of solid waste once it has been gathered.

Smaller municipalities and rural towns, however, generally have no centralized solid waste management system, and individuals must dispose of any trash they generate. Because, as will be illustrated in Excerpts 2 and 3 and Figure 5.4, in Nicaragua there is a value for "clean," swept areas clear of debris, individuals tend to clear trash daily from areas seen as their responsibility, such as homes, yards, and business fronts. However, areas that are not clearly under the care of an individual or a business can accumulate inorganic waste – such as bags, bottles, and other packaging – and organic waste – like sticks and fallen leaves. The accumulated inorganic waste causes environmental problems by accumulating in arroyos and lakes and public health issues, as rainwater can collect in discarded receptacles and provide a breeding ground for mosquitoes carrying harmful diseases like dengue fever, the chikungunya and Zika viruses, and malaria. One solution encouraged by development organizations such as the Peace Corps is for individuals to reuse as much solid waste as possible and bury the rest. This approach is challenging, however, due to the high levels of rainfall in Nicaragua during the wet season. Much of Nicaragua experiences a low percentage of "dry days" – days without any rainfall – during the rainy season (Gourdji, Läderach, Valle, Martinez, & Lobell, 2015), and pits created for trash disposal therefore often

Figure 5.1 Community members sweeping materials into piles to be burned at a community "clean-up"

(Photo taken by author)

fill with water. Since solid waste burial sites that collect standing water are vulnerable to the same public health hazards as discarded trash, burying trash becomes impractical for five to six months of the year in most of Nicaragua. As a result, the widespread custom in rural areas is to burn the trash gathered in one's own home and to immediately discard any waste – such as food and drink packaging – generated while outside of the home. Community members will then often meet for weekly "clean-ups" in which trash and organic debris in public areas is swept into piles and burned (as in Figure 5.1).

Data and methodology

This chapter takes an ethnographic and discourse analytic approach to the analysis of culturally relevant values in environmental communication theory and practice. Data were collected from 20 ethnographic interviews – loosely structured in-depth interviews – 15 hours of recorded participant observation of environmental and everyday activities, photo documentation, and archival analysis. The primary data collection site was a town which I give the pseudonym Los Llanos (Figure 5.2). Los Llanos is located in the municipality of Ciudad Darío in the central Nicaraguan department of Matagalpa. It is situated in what was historically a tropical dry forest, though widespread deforestation has caused substantial erosion, soil degradation, and local climactic changes (Gourdji et al., 2015). The town consists of around 1,000 inhabitants living in approximately 120 houses, and is located 70 kilometers north of Managua. The eastern edge of Los Llanos borders the Pan-American Highway, making Managua and the department capital of Matagalpa fairly accessible to community members. While many residents of Los Llanos thus work near Managua in clothing factories or meat processing plants, the majority are subsistence farmers who cultivate corn, beans, squash, tomatoes, and onions. Families typically have chickens, pigs, dogs, and cats, and in addition occasionally have turkeys, ducks, horses, or cows. Hurricane Mitch significantly affected this central department of Matagalpa in 1998, causing severe flooding and substantial loss of life and property (Cupples, 2007). Since that disaster, Los Llanos has experienced considerable involvement from international NGOs – some forming longstanding relationships in the community that last years, and

Figure 5.2 A house in the community of Los Llanos, Nicaragua
(Photo taken by author)

others creating shorter term involvements in which their presence in the community ends after the completion of one project.

From 2010 to 2013 I lived in the community of Los Llanos while serving as an Environmental Educator with the Peace Corps. I taught elementary-level science classes and promoted community gardens, nurseries, recycling, and other trash management strategies. This experience allowed me to build relationships with community members and understand the local cultural environmental values in an ethnographic way. It also provided the context through which community members interacted with me as a researcher in 2014. When conducting ethnographic interviews surrounding environmental practices and values, for instance, participants often self-corrected, mindful of our past relationships and my former position as an environmental educator and development worker.

The data analyzed in this chapter come primarily from three sources. The first is documents and public statements surrounding a national environmental education campaign launched by the Sandinista government in 2013. The second source of data comes from photographs of a visual environmental education campaign carried out by elementary educators in a community near Los Llanos. The third source is ethnographic interviews conducted with community members, many of which were completed while the interviewees participated in environmental activities.

Analysis

Estrategia Nacional Para Vivir Limpio, Vivir Sano, Vivir Bonito, Vivir Bien . . .!

In 2013 the Nicaraguan government introduced a national campaign to improve the health and safety of communities, called the *Estrategia Nacional para Vivir Limpio, Vivir Sano, Vivir Bonito, Vivir Bien . . .!* ("the National Strategy for Living Cleanly, Living Healthily, Living Beautifully, Living Well . . .!"). This campaign was introduced by the First Lady Rosario Murillo (the wife of President Daniel Ortega) via a televised broadcast on January 22, 2013 and was then reprinted in many of the national newspapers. The campaign's colorful logo, which proclaimed "Yo vivo bonito!" ("I live beautifully!") and depicted a man and woman holding a baby in front of an idyllic house, was seen frequently on promotional materials. T-shirts, posters, and bumper stickers were distributed widely, and schools were given corresponding age-appropriate activities to promote the *Estrategia Nacional* in the classroom.

The following excerpt is taken from the televised interview with Murillo in which she introduces the initiation of the campaign. In it she describes the goals and purpose of the national endeavor.

Excerpt 1

Qué hermoso va a ser ver los frutos de esta labor que tiene que ser infatigable, incansable, cotidiana, de creación y consolidación de valores; vivir en armonía con la naturaleza, con la Madre Tierra, vivir procurando Bien Común, vivir desde la persona, la familia y la comunidad en conexión permanente con el infinito, con Dios Nuestro Señor, con nuestros valores, con nuestras creencias; promover ese ambiente familiar y comunitario limpio, sano, digno, que genera confianza, optimismo, alegría y procura prosperidad. Todas esas son las búsquedas de esta propuesta, de este modelo de trabajo en responsabilidad compartida, en solidaridad y complementariedad, entendiendo que en la unión, en la Unidad, en la Fraternidad esta la Fuerza, la Fortaleza que nos impulsa hacia adelante.

Television announcement by Rosario Murillo on January 22, 2012, reprinted online by El 19:[1]

How beautiful it will be to see the fruits of this labor – which needs to be tireless, continuous, and daily – of the creation and consolidation of values; to live in harmony with nature, with Mother Earth, to live ensuring the common good, to live connected personally, as a family and as a community, with the infinite, with God our savior, with our values, with our beliefs; to promote for our families and communities an atmosphere of cleanliness, health, and dignity, that creates trust, optimism, happiness, and prosperity. All these are the goals of the proposal, that out of this model of work with shared responsibility, in solidarity and complementarity, understanding that in this union, in this togetherness, in this brotherhood is the force, the strength that pushes us forward. (Author's translation)

In this interview, Murillo introduces the campaign as explicitly about the "creación y consolidación de valores" ("the creation and consolidation of values"), which she goes on to elaborate as "vivir en armonía con la naturaleza, con la Madre Tierra, vivir procurando Bien Común, vivir . . . en conexión permanente con Dios Nuestro Señor" ("to live in harmony with nature, with Mother Earth, to live ensuring the common good, to live connected . . . with God our savior"). Murillo places each of these values in a parallel structure, positioning them as parts of the same ultimate aim.

The next segment, which comes from the text of the original document describing the *Estrategia Nacional*, elaborates further on what it means, exactly, to *Vivir Limpio, Vivir Sano, Vivir Bonito, Vivir Bien*.

Excerpt 2

Nos invitamos, nos convocamos, a trabajar junt@s, a aprender junt@s, nicaragüenses de todas las generaciones, para transformar nuestra

Cultura de la Vida Cotidiana, poniendo los énfasis indispensables en la coherencia entre lo que somos, lo que pensamos, y lo que hacemos.

Vivir Limpio, Vivir Sano, Vivir Bonito, Vivir Bien . . .! Significa para cada un@ de nosotr@s, emprender junt@s una serie de Acciones simples, sencillas, diarias, que vayan incorporándonos a una Conciencia de Responsabilidad Compartida y Complementaria sobre el País que soñamos, y el País, la Sociedad, la Comunidad, la Familia y el Ser Humano, que queremos re-crear para Bien. Para Mejor. Para que Nicaragua continúe siendo Ejemplo Iluminado, de Idiosincrasia, Identidad, Inteligencia, Sensibilidad y Prácticas, que desde el corazón representen contribución esencial al Mundo Mejor que entre tod@s estamos obligad@s a hacer posible.

. . .

GUIA BASICA PARA VIVIR LIMPIO, VIVIR SANO, VIVIR BONITO, VIVIR BIEN . . .!

1. Aprendamos junt@s desde la Familia, la Comunidad, la Escuela, con el acompañamiento, la promoción y facilitación de las Instituciones del Estado, las Iglesias, la Empresa Privada, l@s Productor@s, Normas sencillas y prácticas de Convivencia entre nosotr@s; entre nosotr@s, la Naturaleza y la Madre Tierra; y entre Espacios Familiares y Comunitarios, Públicos y Privados, donde observemos Limpieza, Higiene, Orden, Estética, Respeto, Cuido Amoroso y Solidaridad Permanente.

. . .

4. Sembremos árboles, plantas, huertos, hierbas de cocina y medicinales, en todos los espacios urbanos, suburbanos y de Vivienda Rural, de manera que apuntemos a cuidar y restaurar a nuestra Madre Tierra y a cuidarnos nosotr@s mismos, consumiendo lo que producimos localmente, abasteciéndonos, en gran parte, de temporada en temporada, de una producción local saludable, que también fortalezca Buenas Prácticas de Agricultura Familiar y Comunitaria.

Así estaremos consolidando la Salud de la Madre Tierra y de todas las generaciones de nicaragüenses, que sabemos vivir con Fé. L@s nicaragüenses vivimos con Valores. Con Cariño expresado en fuertes vínculos con la Madre Tierra. En Vínculos de Familia. En lazos de Comunidad, Cultura, Religiosidad y Tradición, así como de nuestra propia Cultura Culinaria, Herbolaria, Medicinal, y de Alimentación. Tenemos tanta riqueza cultural que nos toca admirar, cuidar y conservar como Tesoro.

Document released by the Sandinista government January 25, 2013, reprinted online by El 19:[2]

We are invited, we are called, to work together, to learn together, Nicaraguans from all generations, to transform the culture of our daily life, putting an indispensable emphasis on consistency between what we are, what we think, and what we do.

Live cleanly, live healthily, live beautifully, live well . . .! That means for each of us to carry out together a series of basic, simple, daily actions that continue incorporating us into a conscience of responsibility both shared and complementary about the country of which we dream, and the country, the society, the community, the family and humanity that we want to recreate for the better. For the best. So that Nicaragua continues to be an illuminating example of traits, identity, intelligence, sensitivity and practices, that represent an essential contribution from the heart to a better world that we are all obligated to make possible.

. . .

BASIC GUIDE FOR LIVING CLEANLY, LIVING HEALTHILY, LIVING BEAUTIFULLY, LIVING WELL . . .!

1. Let's learn together in our families, our communities, our schools – with the help, the promotion, and the facilitation of the state institutions, the churches, the private businesses, and the farmers – the basic norms and practices of coexistence with each other, between ourselves, nature, and Mother Earth, and in family and community spaces public and private, where we follow cleanliness, hygiene, order, aesthetic, respect, loving care, and permanent solidarity.

. . .

4. Let's plant trees, plants, gardens, and cooking and medicinal herbs in all the urban and suburban spaces and the rural homes, in a way that we volunteer to care for and restore our Mother Earth and take care of ourselves, eating what we produce locally, providing for ourselves, in large part, from season to season, from a local, healthy production that will also strengthen good practices for family and community agriculture.

In this way we will be strengthening the health of Mother Earth and of all the generations of Nicaraguans, who know how to live with faith. Nicaraguans live with values. With care expressed through strong bonds with Mother Earth. Through family bonds. Through community ties, culture, religiousness and tradition, such as our own culinary, herbal, medicinal, and nutritional culture. We have so much cultural richness that we must admire, care for, and conserve as a treasure. (Author's translation)

This text also explicitly aims to reinforce values, proclaiming that the purpose of the *Estrategia* is "la coherencia entre lo que somos, lo que pensamos, y lo que hacemos," ("the consistency between what we are, what we think, and what we do") and that "L@s nicaragüenses vivimos con Valores" ("Nicaraguans live with values"). The text goes on to describe the promoted value system in which an orientation to environmentalism is intrinsically linked with the protection of public health, the maintenance of clean, hygienic community spaces, and respect for religious and political institutions. The first bullet point, for instance, addresses behaviors that will promote "Normas sencillas y prácticas de Convivencia entre nosotr@s; entre nosotr@s, la Naturaleza y la Madre Tierra" ("basic norms and practices of coexistence with each other, between ourselves, nature, and Mother Earth"). Among the norms suggested by the campaign to coexist well with nature and Mother Earth is maintaining, in both public and private spaces, "Limpieza, Higiene, Orden, Estética, Respeto, Cuido Amoroso y Solidaridad Permanente" ("cleanliness, hygiene, order, aesthetic, respect, loving care, and permanent solidarity"). The fourth bullet point, furthermore, suggests that by planting trees and gardens in public spaces, community members can learn "a cuidar y restaurar a nuestra Madre Tierra y a cuidarnos nosotr@s mismos" ("to care for and restore our Mother Earth and to take care of ourselves"), which they will do by eating locally produced, healthy food. The system of values illustrated explicitly links environmental, aesthetic, public health, religious, and political values, placing them as all aspects of one moral set. The inclusion of environmental values as part of this value system differs from Westernized environmental value systems in several ways. Murillo creates no dichotomy or any distinction, for example, between benefit to the environment and benefit to humans. This set of values also places much greater emphasis on public health and aesthetic public spaces than Westernized environmental value systems. Finally, the link between environmental values and Christian religious values differs from previous research which argues that some Judeo-Christian religions encourage anthropocentric views of the environment (Schultz, Zelezny, & Dalrymple, 2000; White, 1967), although other scholars have asserted that Christian and environmental values can be complementary in Westernized contexts as well (Northcott, 2016).

The inseparability of cleared, well-tended spaces, the safeguarding of public health, and the protection of the environment which is demonstrated by the text of the *Estrategia Nacional* is also explicitly illustrated by many of the educational materials distributed to schools as part of the campaign. One such educational pamphlet, for instance, is titled "que debemos hacer para vivir limpios, vivir sanos, vivir bonito, vivir bien" ("what we should do to live cleanly, live healthily, live beautifully, live well"). The flyer, beneath the heading "Nicaragua, Cristiana, Socialista, y Solidaria" ("Nicaragua, Christian, Socialist, and Solidary"), illustrates what it means to carry out the values of the *Estrategia Nacional* with a childlike drawing of two children picking up trash from the immaculate front yard of a small house. Beneath the drawing, the caption implores that we "cuidemos Nicaragua" ("take care of Nicaragua"), presumably by following the illustrated children's example and collecting solid waste. Creating a "clean" community is thus promoted as part of a bundle of positively evaluated characteristics for a community, alongside dignity and health, and more broadly, Christian and socialist values; the creation of this clean community is then portrayed practically as the personal obligation to participate in waste management strategies.

It is also not uncommon to see the linked values of environmental protection, cleanliness, and public health in other visual messages throughout Nicaragua. Many signs and painted slogans around Managua, for instance, declare *Managua limpia, Ciudad sana,* ("A clean Managua is a healthy Managua"), illustrating and reinforcing the connection between cleanliness, environmental protection, and public health, and re-establishing the culturally specific value system in which environmental values are situated.

Local environmental campaign

The next case study illustrates the mobilization of this value system in the grassroots environmental education context – a campaign created by teachers at a public elementary school near Los Llanos. In the small rural Nicaraguan communities of this area, elementary schools generally consist of one to three connected classrooms. The buildings are painted blue on the lower half, white on the upper part, and surrounded by a dirt and grass schoolyard. Students keep the yard tidy by trimming the grass with machetes and frequently sweeping the bare dirt areas. Often the school's latrines are located at the far edge of the schoolyard and consist of a concrete base, a concrete seat over the latrine pit, a metal frame, and tin walls and roof (Figure 5.3). Because illness can be spread from the fecal matter in the latrines by flies and other insects, in some latrines, such as the one in Figure 5.3, a flat material will be placed on the seat as a cover for the aperture. This cover must be removed before the latrine is used and replaced afterwards. The campaign examined in this chapter was designed to encourage students to place the improvised lid back on the latrine seat after every use.

Figure 5.3 shows the inside of a school latrine which has been illustrated as part of an environmental campaign created by local teachers. The message reads "Cuidemos de nuestro medio ambiente tapando las letrinas" ("protect our environment by putting lids on the latrines"), and above the message is a drawing of rocks and grass, presumably representing the schoolyard. This message urges students to cover the latrine after every use to prevent flies and further disease vectors from spreading parasites and other illnesses which might be found in the fecal matter inside the latrine pit. In this

Figure 5.3 Environmental education message: "Protect our environment by putting
     lids on the latrines"

(Photo taken by author)

illustration the value of environmental protection has a clear and bounded
space – the immediate physical environment of the school – and its goals
align exactly with those of assuring the public health through clean environments. Although this activity may not be considered a pro-environmental
behavior in many Westernized approaches, in rural Nicaragua it is seen by
community members as such, fitting within the value system in which protecting the environment and protecting public health are inseparable.

Reflection on community clean-up

The differences between westernized US American and Nicaraguan cultural value systems become especially salient in environmental communication interactions between international NGO workers – usually European-American second-language Spanish speakers – and local Nicaraguan community members. One example of this phenomenon is illustrated in the waste management activities and ideologies of the community members from the town in which I lived as a Peace Corps volunteer. In Los Llanos, Matagalpa, community members meet weekly to sweep up and burn any fallen material in the streets, including paper, plastic bags and bottles, chip and other snack bags, leaves, sticks, and other organic and inorganic materials. Members of each household, including children, sweep fallen materials into small piles about 20 feet apart, then set them on fire, often carrying a piece of trash from an already burning pile to an unlit pile to conserve matches.

While it could be argued that this activity is detrimental to both environmental and public health, Los Llanos community members view their actions as beneficial to the environment and attribute their adoption of the practice to environmental trainings given by international NGOs. In the following excerpt from an ethnographic interview, for instance, María explains the community's rationale for the activity as necessary for public health and for making the community look *limpia* ("clean") – something that she sees as critical for environmental protection. The following excerpt was recorded while María participated in a weekly community clean-up.

Excerpt 3

1 Jessi:	¿Por qué es importante la limpieza?	*Why is cleaning important?*
2 María:	Bueno, esta limpieza es importante para la salud,	*Well, this cleaning is important for health,*
3	y también para que el medio ambiente	*and also so that the environment*
4	se mire limpio,	*looks clean,*
5	porque usted se imagina, que todo sucio eso,	*because imagine, all this dirty,*
6	se mira feo.	*it looks ugly.*
7	Entonces por eso nos proponemos en,	*That's why we do this,*
8	ponemos interés en la limpieza.	*emphasize the cleaning.*
9	Hasta ahora lo han explicado mejor,	*Now they've explained better,*

10	estos organismos, los que han venido de-,	*those organizations that have come from-,*
11	el Arco Iris, El Porvenir,	*the Rainbow Network, El Porvenir,*
12	ustedes, que también vienen de extranjero,	*you guys, that also come from overseas,*
13	a dar buenas orientaciones,	*to give good trainings,*
14	del medio ambiente, salud.	*about the environment, health.*
15	Eso hacemos nosotros.	*That's what we do.*

Here the two justifications that María provides for the *limpieza* ("clean-up") draw on local value systems. In line 2, for instance she says "esta limpieza es importante para la salud" ("this clean-up is important for health reasons") and in lines 3–4 she says "y tambien para que el medio ambiente se mire limpio" ("and also so that the environment looks clean"). In these explanations María illustrates the same value systems shown in Excerpts 1 and 2: environmental protection shares a social meaning, and the associated individual behaviors, with protecting the public health, maintaining aesthetically pleasing communities, and upholding community order and hygiene. As in the local environmental education campaign, the environment, for María, is the immediate and bounded physical surroundings. While words such as "bonito" ("pretty") and "feo" ("ugly") are also used in Nicaraguan Spanish as more colloquial synonyms for "good" and "bad," here María draws on aesthetic values for the clean, swept spaces seen in Figure 5.4. She illustrates and reinforces the network of cultural values seen in the *Estrategia Nacional Para Vivir Limpio, Vivir Sano, Vivir Bonito, Vivir Bien . . .!*; here, to live cleanly and healthily is to live beautifully as well. Crucially, María explicitly attributes the community clean-up, and its environmental and public health motivations, to contact with foreign organizations which, in her interpretation, have given *buenas orientaciones* ("good trainings") to the community about the importance of cleanliness for both health and the environment. In lines 9–14 she says, "hasta ahora lo han explicado mejor, o, los que han entrado, estos organismos, los que han venido de, el Arco Eris, El Porvenir, ustedes, que también vienen del extranjero, a dar buenas orientaciones, del medio ambiente, salud" ("Now they've explained better, those organizations, the ones that have come from, Arco Iris, El Porvenir, you guys, that also come from overseas, to give us good trainings, about the environment, health").

It is also important to note that this interview took place with the author, who had an existing relationship with community members as a development worker. This relationship is clearly salient in the interview. María

Figure 5.4 Hygienically clean (swept bare) yards in Los Llanos, Nicaragua
(Photo taken by author)

mentions, for instance, that NGOs have recently explained better how the community should act with respect to the environment and health, and self-corrects at one point, pausing, and then including *ustedes* ("you guys") in her list of organizations that had organized trainings. It should also be noted that creating video-recorded messages of gratitude was a genre familiar to María and other community members, as NGOs often request these videos as a way to recognize and report to donors in the United States and other countries. It is notable, however, that despite clearly adjusting her response to say what she expected I, as a former international environmental educator, would want to hear, María still interprets burning trash as a pro-environmental behavior, although it was a practice which I attempted to discourage while living in Los Llanos. Despite attributing the community's actions to trainings from foreign organizations, María draws on very local values and moral judgments when she says "usted se imagina, que todo sucio esto, se mira feo" (lines 5–6: "imagine, if all of this were dirty, it would look ugly"). By interpreting new environmental education through her existing value systems, María positions the practice of burning trash as a pro-environmental behavior congruent with the system of environmental values held by the community, and furthermore interprets the existing community practice of burning trash as the pro-environmental behaviors promoted by international organizations.

Discussion

This chapter analyzes environmental discourses and values at three levels. The first is a nationwide campaign carried out through television and other mass media, the second is a local, grassroots environmental message created by teachers in a rural school, and the third is an individual reflection on the goals of an environmental activity. At each of these levels community members draw on environmental values as elements of a culturally specific bundle of values. In Nicaragua that value system consists of a focus on the "cleanliness" of spaces, protecting the environment, respecting governmental and religious institutions, and preserving the public health. In the first context, the *Estrategia Nacional*, the title explicitly states the values as *vivir limpio, vivir sano, vivir bonito, vivir bien* ("living cleanly, living healthily, living beautifully, living well"), and although the term "environment" is not specifically stated in the title, living in harmony with nature is the first stated goal of the campaign, which was created primarily to tackle issues of solid waste disposal (Nading & Fisher, 2017). The second and third examples analyzed in this chapter continue to demonstrate the intrinsic relationships between these values for community members. The environmental education message, for instance, illustrates that, for local teachers and students, protecting the environment and protecting public health are not separate objectives, but fundamentally part of the same goal. The third context, a participant's reflection on the purpose of a common environmental activity, shows how cultural value systems can impact environmental communication. In the case of the Los Llanos community clean-up, for instance, because community members interpreted environmental education and suggestions from international NGOs within a locally relevant system of values, they interpreted the environmental training very differently than it was intended. The incongruity had a damaging effect, as the environmental trainings eventually reinforced a practice that has detrimental consequences for both the environment and public health.

The environmental values observed in these Nicaraguan contexts show some similarities with descriptions of the values systems of US Latinos. A division between humanity and nature is largely absent in this cultural context, for instance, and stewardship of utilitarian land is seen as an important focus of environmental protection. This echoes Lynch's analysis, "For most US Latinos, Walden Pond and Glen Canyon are less crucial as referents than the fruit and vegetable farms of California's Central Valley, the grazing lands of the arid Southwest, the hillside farms of Puerto Rico and the Dominican Republic, and Caribbean fisheries" (1993, p. 119). Some aspects of the value systems differ, however. For example, while the rejection of US imperialism and capitalism are frequent features of the Sandinista government's discourse, they are not values found in the same system with environmental conservation, cleanliness, and the protection of public health, differing from Peña's observation among US Latinos in the Southwest (2005a, 2005b).

The cultural value systems observed in this chapter may also interact with other measures of environmental beliefs. In Nicaragua, for instance, Schultz and Zelezny (1998) found that the NEP did not significantly predict pro-environmental behavior. One potential explanation for this finding is that the NEP's focus on environmental conservation for ecocentric reasons is incompatible with the value system held by many Nicaraguans, where the goals of protecting the environment overlap largely with public health goals, maintaining institutions, and creating a hygienic and aesthetic community. A self-transcendence measure, though, may be more compatible with the bundle of values in Los Llanos, and Schultz and Zelezny (1998) did find it to be predictive of pro-environmental behaviors among Nicaraguan college students. There are a few crucial differences between Schultz and Zelezny's participants and the community of Los Llanos, however. Schultz and Zelezny's participants were all college students, for instance, who tend to be more economically privileged than most Nicaraguans. The college was also in an urban center, where many environmental behaviors and issues differ from more rural areas. Finally, it is important to note that environmental behavioral choices may differ widely across cultural boundaries. In rural Nicaragua, for instance, very few people have access to private vehicles, and the standard transportation is through public busses. Conserving water and electricity, while helpful to the local environment, may also be seen more as economic choices than environmental ones. In Los Llanos, for example, electricity has only recently become available to residents, and still represents a significant expense to households. Additionally, while a public, mechanically pumped water project was completed in 2011, water availability is rotated and unpredictable. Residents are therefore extremely conservative with water. If household stores of water run out, they have to obtain more by hand from the limited number of wells in the community. Behavioral choices that relate to the environmental concerns associated with farming methods, trash disposal, firewood collection, cookstove material, and pesticide use, among others, would be more relevant measures of pro-environmental behaviors for the residents of Los Llanos, though they are not consistent with the pro-environmental behavioral choices faced by

US residents. Furthermore, even within a relatively small country like Nicaragua, the locally relevant environmental behavioral choices may differ widely, creating a substantial limitation to cross-cultural and international survey research of environmental behaviors.

In this chapter I argue that, in order to understand environmental beliefs and behaviors in cross-cultural contexts, environmental communication researchers must develop an ethnographic understanding of the environmental values and behaviors within the community of study. Furthermore, I contend that environmental values in Nicaragua are not isolated, but rather linked with other salient values toward public health, religious and political institutions, and the cleanliness of communities. In each of the contexts observed, from national, governmental discourse to local, grassroots messages, environmental values are constructed as inseparable from public health and aesthetic values. This intrinsic connection becomes especially salient in a context of cross-cultural environmental communication, where an environmental message about trash management is interpreted through the local value system and seen as an endorsement of, and encouragement to, burn all discarded items, including plastic packaging, vehicle tires, and other toxic materials. I thus argue that to successfully understand and communicate about environmental problems, both researchers and practitioners must develop an ethnographic understanding of environmental values and the cultural value systems in which they are situated.

As all ethnography necessarily represents a specific time and place, this study is inherently limited to a distinct context. Of the numerous environmental education campaigns being conducted in rural Nicaragua, this study considers only three and does not claim to speak more broadly. The research was also informed by my previous experience with the research community. There are significant challenges for many researchers when including ethnographic and locally relevant perspectives in studies of environmental communication: scholars may be aiming to collect data from many communities simultaneously, may experience linguistic or financial obstacles, may not be able to physically travel to the community of interest, or may have little time there if they are able to go. Many researchers, however, can still adopt a number of ethnographic methods that allow for the consideration of cultural values and center the perspectives of the participants. Even researchers who are unable to spend enough time in a community to use a methodology such as community-based participatory research (Chen, Milstein, Anguiano, Sandoval, & Knudsen, 2012) may conduct focus group interviews, for instance, or include elicitation tasks (Satterfield, 2001) or a qualitative analysis of longer-form answers in survey-based studies. Researchers can also employ multiple methods or mixed methods in order to not lose sight of the participants and their diverse perspectives when completing larger quantitative or multi-sited projects.

Conclusion

This chapter illustrates the importance of the interaction between cultural values and local understandings of pro-environmental behaviors. It examines the mobilization of environmental values in Nicaragua at three levels: through a national environmental education campaign, a local grassroots environmental education message, and community members' reflections on their behavior as they participate in environmental activities. I argue that, in many of these discourses, environmental values exist in an inseparable bundle with other cultural values, such as an orientation to public health, respect for institutions, and the hygiene of public and private spaces. Many Nicaraguans are among the people who will be disproportionately affected by both local and global environmental crises, but in order to work with the local population to address these impacts, development workers and researchers of intercultural environmental communication need to understand the locally relevant systems of values in which environmental values are positioned. In planning and analyzing environmental communication across racial and cultural contexts, then, researchers can benefit from ethnographic and discourse analytic methodologies to develop this understanding of the local environmental context, and future research on cross-cultural environmental communication should aim to include ethnographic approaches to understanding environmental values. This is especially necessary when different value systems come into contact, a phenomenon that will only become more prevalent as the global community responds to worsening environmental crises.

Notes

1 El 19 Digital. *Estrategia Nacional para "Vivir Limpio, Vivir Sano, Vivir Bonito, Vivir Bien . . .!"*. www.el19digital.com/articulos/ver/titulo:7426-rosario-en-multinoticias-23-de-enero-2013-
2 "Consejo de Comunicación y Ciudadanía". *Rosario en Multinoticias (23 de enero 2013)*. www.el19digital.com/articulos/ver/titulo:7428-estrategia-nacional-para-vivir-limpio-vivir-sano-vivir-bonito-vivir-bien

References

Ardoin, N. M., & Sivek, D. J. (2002). An environmental education needs assessment study in the Carazo department of Nicaragua. *Applied Environmental Education & Communication, 1*(4), 235–244.

Carter, E. D. (2016). Environmental justice 2.0: New Latino environmentalism in Los Angeles. *Local Environment, 21*(1), 3–23.

Chatterjee, D. P. (2008). Oriental disadvantage versus occidental exuberance: Appraising environmental concern in India – A case study in a local context. *International Sociology, 23*(1), 5–33.

Chen, Y., Milstein, T., Anguiano, C., Sandoval, J., & Knudsen, L. (2012). Challenges and benefits of community-based participatory research for environmental justice: A case of collaboratively examining ecocultural struggles. *Environmental Communication: A Journal of Nature and Culture, 6*(3), 403–421.

Corraliza, J. A., & Berenguer, J. (2000). Environmental values, beliefs, and actions: A situational approach. *Environment and Behavior, 32*(6), 832–848.

Corral-Verdugo, V., & Armendáriz, L. I. (2000). The 'New Environmental Paradigm' in a Mexican community. *Journal of Environmental Education, 31*(3), 25–31.

Coupland, N., & Coupland, J. (1997). Bodies, beaches and burn-times: Environmentalism and its discursive competitors. *Discourse & Society, 8*(1), 7–25.

Cupples, J. (2007). Gender and hurricane Mitch: Reconstructing subjectivities after disaster. *Disasters, 31*(2), 155–175.

De Groot, J. I. M., & Steg, L. (2007). Value orientations and environmental beliefs in five countries: Validity of an instrument to measure egoistic, altruistic and biospheric value orientations. *Journal of Cross-Cultural Psychology, 38*(3), 318–332.

Deng, J., Walker, G. J., & Swinnerton, G. (2006). A comparison of environmental values and attitudes between Chinese in Canada and Anglo-Canadians. *Environment and Behavior, 38*(1), 22–47.

Dietz, T., Fitzgerald, A., & Shwom, R. (2005). Environmental values. *Annual Review of Environment and Resources, 30*(1), 335–372.

Dunlap, R. E., & Van Liere, K. D. (1978). The 'New Environmental Paradigm'. *Journal of Environmental Education, 9*(4), 10–19.

Dunlap, R. E., Van Liere, K. D., Mertig, A. G., & Jones, R. E. (2000). New trends in measuring environmental attitudes: Measuring endorsement of the new ecological paradigm: A revised NEP scale. *Journal of Social Issues, 56*(3), 425–442.

Gooch, G. D. (1995). Environmental beliefs and attitudes in Sweden and the Baltic states. *Environment and Behavior, 27*(4), 520–534.

Gourdji, S., Läderach, P., Valle, A. M., Martinez, C. Z., & Lobell, D. B. (2015). Historical climate trends, deforestation, and maize and bean yields in Nicaragua. *Agricultural and Forest Meteorology, 200*, 270–281.

Gromet, D. M., Kunreuther, H., & Larrick, R. P. (2013). Political ideology affects energy-efficiency attitudes and choices. *Proceedings of the National Academy of Sciences, 110*(23), 9314–9319.

Hards, S. (2011). Social practice and the evolution of personal environmental values. *Environmental Values, 20*(1), 23–42.

Hartmann, C. (2018). Waste picker livelihoods and inclusive neoliberal municipal solid waste management policies: The case of the La Chureca garbage dump site in Managua, Nicaragua. *Waste Management, 71*, 565–577.

Herrera, C., Ruben, R., & Dijkstra, G. (2018). Climate variability and vulnerability to poverty in Nicaragua. *Journal of Environmental Economics and Policy*, 1–21.

Hoelle, J. (2017). Jungle beef: Consumption, production and destruction, and the development process in the Brazilian Amazon. *Journal of Political Ecology, 24*(1), 743–762.

Hoornweg, D., & Bhada-Tata, P. (2012). *What a waste: A global review of solid waste management*. Washington, DC: The World Bank.

Ives, C. D., & Kendal, D. (2014). The role of social values in the management of ecological systems. *Journal of Environmental Management, 144*, 67–72.

Johnson, C. Y., Bowker, J. M., & Cordell, H. K. (2004). Ethnic variation in environmental belief and behavior: An examination of the New Ecological Paradigm in a social psychological context. *Environment and Behavior, 36*(2), 157–186.

Kempton, W., Boster, J. S., & Hartley, J. A. (1996). *Environmental values in American culture*. Cambridge, MA: MIT Press.

Kreft, S., & Eckstein, D. (2014). *Global climate risk index*. German Watch, Briefing Paper No. 9, Bonn, Germany.

Lakoff, G. (2010). Why it matters how we frame the environment. *Environmental Communication, 4*(1), 70–81.

Leung, C., & Rice, J. (2002). Comparison of Chinese-Australian and Anglo-Australian environmental attitudes and behavior. *Social Behavior and Personality: An International Journal, 30*(3), 251–262.

Lin, T. T. (2012). Cross-platform framing and cross-cultural adaptation: Examining elephant conservation in Thailand. *Environmental Communication: A Journal of Nature and Culture, 6*(2), 193–211.

Lo, C. W., Fryxell, G. E., & Wong, W. W. (2006). Effective regulations with little effect? The antecedents of the perceptions of environmental officials on enforcement effectiveness in China. *Environmental Management, 38*, 388–410.

Lynch, B. D. (1993). The garden and the sea: U.S. Latino environmental discourses and mainstream environmentalism. *Social Problems, 40*(1), 108–124.

Mayer, F. S., & Frantz, C. M. (2004). The connectedness to nature scale: A measure of individuals' feeling in community with nature. *Journal of Environmental Psychology, 24*(4), 503–515.

Miller, C. A. (2000). The dynamics of framing environmental values and policy: Four models of societal processes. *Environmental Values, 9*(2), 211–233.

Nading, A. M., & Fisher, J. (2017). Zopilotes, alacranes, y hormigas (Vultures, scorpions, and ants): Animal metaphors as organizational politics in a Nicaraguan garbage crisis. *Antipode*, 1–19.

Noe, F. P., & Snow, R. (1990). Hispanic cultural influence on environmental concern. *The Journal of Environmental Education, 21*(2), 27–34.

Northcott, M. S. (2016). Lynn White Jr. right and wrong: The anti-ecological character of Latin Christianity and the pro-ecological turn of protestantism. In T. LeVasseur & A. Peterson (Eds.), *Religion and ecological crisis* (pp. 69–82). London: Routledge.

Peña, D. G. (2005a). *Mexican Americans and the environment: Tierra y vida*. Tucson, AZ: University of Arizona Press.

Peña, D. G. (2005b). Tierra y vida: Chicano environmental justice struggles in the Southwest. In R. D. Bullard (Ed.), *The quest for environmental justice: Human rights and the politics of pollution* (pp. 188–206). San Francisco, CA: Sierra Club Books.

Pierce, J. C., Lovrich, N. P., Jr., Tsurutani, T., & Abe, T. (1986). Culture, politics and mass publics: Traditional and modern supporters of the New Environmental Paradigm in Japan and the United States. *Journal of Politics, 49*, 54–79.

Price, J. C., Walker, I. A., & Boschetti, F. (2014). Measuring cultural values and beliefs about environment to identify their role in climate change responses. *Journal of Environmental Psychology, 37*, 8–20.

Satterfield, T. (2001). In search of value literacy: Suggestions for the elicitation of environmental values. *Environmental Values, 10*(3), 331–359.

Schultz, P. W., Unipan, J. B., & Gamba, R. J. (2000). Acculturation and ecological worldview among Latino Americans. *The Journal of Environmental Education, 31*(2), 22–27.

Schultz, P. W., & Zelezny, L. C. (1998). Values and proenvironmental behavior. *Journal of Cross-Cultural Psychology, 29*(4), 540–558.

Schultz, P. W., Zelezny, L. C., & Dalrymple, N. J. (2000). A multinational perspective on the relation between Judeo-Christian religious beliefs and attitudes of environmental concern. *Environment and Behavior, 32*(4), 576–591.

Schwartz, S. H. (1977). Normative influences on altruism. *Advances in Experimental Social Psychology, 10*, 221–279.

Schwartz, S. H. (1992). Universals in the content and structure of values: Theoretical advances and empirical tests in 20 countries. *Advances in Experimental Social Psychology, 25*(1), 1–65.

Schwartz, S. H. (1994). Are there universal aspects in the structure and contents of human values? *Journal of Social Issues, 50*(4), 19–45.

Schwartz, S. H., & Bilsky, W. (1987). Toward a universal psychological structure of human values. *Journal of Personality and Social Psychology, 53*(3), 550–562.

Shin, W. S. (2001). Reliability and factor structure of a Korean version of the New Environmental Paradigm. *Journal of Social Behavior and Personality, 16*(1), 9–18.

Stern, P. C., & Dietz, T. (1994). The value basis of environmental concern. *Journal of Social Issues, 50*, 65–84.

Stern, P. C., Dietz, T., Abel, T., Guagnano, G. A., & Kalof, L. (1999). A value-belief-norm theory of support for social movements: The case of environmental concern. *Human Ecology Review, 6*, 81–97.

Stern, P. C., Dietz, T., Kalof, L., & Guagnano, G. A. (1995). Values, beliefs, and proenvironmental action: Attitude formation toward emergent attitude objects. *Journal of Applied Social Psychology, 25*, 1611–1636.

Thompson, S. C., & Barton, M. A. (1994). Ecocentric and anthropocentric attitudes toward the environment. *Journal of Environmental Psychology, 14*(2), 149–157.

White, L., Jr. (1967). The historical roots of our ecological crisis. *Science, 155*(3767), 1203–1207.

6 Women farmers' voices on climate change adaptation in India

Jagadish Thaker and Mohan J. Dutta

Women farmers' voices on climate change adaptation in India

Adaptation to climate change refers to adjustment in natural or human systems to mitigate the negative impacts of climate change and to foster beneficial opportunities, if any (IPCC, n.d.). Poor women in developing and underdeveloped countries are considered to be more vulnerable to climate change impacts due to the differential global patterns of climate change patterns, cultural norms about gender roles, and increasing gender-based inequalities in access to and control over resources (e.g., Goh, 2012; Kakota, Nyariki, Mkwambisi, & Kogi-Makau, 2011). Moreover, poor and marginalized communities are unfairly burdened with a problem they did not cause, with important gender and ethical implications in conceptualizing who and what constitutes the climate change problem and solutions (Buck, Gammon, & Preston, 2014; Cuomo, 2011; Terry, 2009).

Gender-differentiated impacts of climate change, however, are not always rigid, straightforward, or predictable (Goh, 2012, p. 18; Arora-Jonsson, 2011). For example, portrayals of women as primarily vulnerable in relation to environmental issues deflect attention away from the inequalities that cause such problems in the first place, and subsequent inequalities in developing solutions (Arora-Jonsson, 2011). This lack of opportunities for equal participation in decision-making processes can perpetuate gender inequalities and increase the vulnerability of women (Bee, Biermann, & Tschakert, 2013). Research on climate change adaptation provides an opportunity "to address some of the mistakes and shortcomings of conventional social and economic development pathways that have contributed to social inequity, poverty, and environmental problems" (Eriksen et al., 2011, p. 8).

To do that, adaptation to climate change needs to be situated within the prevailing relations of power and decision-making processes: how is the problem of climate change adaptation constituted, who makes the decisions, and what are the effects of such decisions on different social strata

(Carr, 2008)? For example, Eriksen, Brown, and Kelly (2005), who examined drought-affected smallholder communities in Tanzania and Kenya, suggested that adaptation strategies can perpetuate women's disadvantages, as the policies tend to favor men who have better access to information and institutional support. In other words, adaptation policies that do not address existing gender norms and roles are most likely to perpetuate the prevailing gender inequities (Tschakert & Machado, 2012).

This chapter answers the call to link the extensive climate change vulnerability and adaptation literature with feminist scholarship on how gender is a critical factor in understanding environmental change, conflict, and management (e.g., Arora-Jonsson, 2011; Bee et al., 2013). It presents the results of a project using a participatory research approach by co-constructing meanings of climate change and adaptation options along with a collective of Dalit women farmers. Dalit refers to the most discriminated caste in Indian and few Asian communities, marked by low socioeconomic status. The study focused on Dalit women farmers' experiences about climate change, their current adaptation practices, and the barriers they say hinder their adaptation strategies. By focusing on the lived experiences, this chapter argues that top-down formulations of vulnerability and adaptation solutions, such as promotion of genetically modified (GM) crops, further marginalize the concerns and indigenous knowledge systems of the vulnerable segments in society.

Culture, structure, and climate change adaptation

Feminist philosophers have argued that climate change is overtly framed in Western scientific-technology terms, as objective, value-neutral, and free of social and cultural contexts (see Israel & Sachs, 2013; Moosa & Tuana, 2014). For example, context-free scientific frames of the climate change problem, such as an informal target to limit global temperature rise to two degrees (see Seager, 2009), obfuscates differential responsibility and impacts of climate change, not only between the global industrialized North and the global South, but also within regions and nations. These scientific-technical discourses critically ignore alternative cultural and contextual epistemologies that shape how people make sense of and respond to climate change. Responding to the call to "start off research from women's lives in households" to build alternative epistemologies of sciences (Harding, 2008, p. 225), this chapter builds on how climate change impacts are understood by poor women farmers in a semi-arid region in India.

Women's vulnerability and agency

Feminist scholars have argued that constructing poor women in the global South as victims or virtuous in relation to environmental problems conceals unequal power structures that are the primary drivers of vulnerability, and displaces critical questions about power, access, impacts, and rights (Arora-Jonsson, 2011; Bee et al., 2013). On the one hand, women in the global South are projected as "one dimensional objects" (MacGregor, 2010, p. 227) and are portrayed as helpless, voiceless subjects who are unable to cope without the help of large development organizations. On the other hand, women are projected as virtuous and are increasingly held responsible for facilitating better adaptation in communities, embodying the feminization of responsibility (Arora-Jonsson, 2011). Such disempowering discourses "can be and have been used to legitimize the imposition of external, top-down interventions to 'effectively' tackle climate change, further marginalizing and silencing women's . . . voices and their experiences in dealing with climatic extremes" (Bee et al., 2013, p. 98).

To better understand the political economy of adaptation policies, it is important to situate the climate change adaptation discourses within the contexts of feminist, postcolonial, and subaltern critiques to guide how scientific issues such as climate change get addressed in social, economic, and political terms within subaltern communities of women. Situated in this backdrop, scholars can foster spaces for social change by working in solidarity with subaltern communities to co-create entry points to develop local as well as international-level climate change solutions.

Structural determinants of vulnerability in agriculture

The dominant discourse in the adaptation literature suggests there are several technology adaptation options readily available to solve climate change. In this frame, the traditional role of scholars is to identify the social and cultural barriers to implementing these adaptation actions (Rogers, 2003; Tschakert & Machado, 2012). For example, governments and corporations have promoted GM crops such as Bt cotton as a solution to the agriculture crisis (Glover, 2010a, 2010b; Qaim, 2010; Qaim & Kouser, 2013). Bt cotton refers to an insect-resistant transgenic crop that expresses a microbial protein from the bacterium Bacillus thuringiensis. Recently, GM crops have been promoted as a successful adaptation strategy for farmers (Qaim & Kouser, 2013; Zilberman, 2014). Various studies, however, indicate the differential benefits to Bt cotton farmers, with poor farmers at high risk due to high investments and varying returns due to changing market prices (Crost, Shankar, Bennett, & Morse, 2007; Glover, 2010a, 2010b; Morse, Mannion, & Evans, 2012; Stone, 2010).

There is increasing scholarly work pointing to structural factors, such as access to resources and institutions, which play critical roles in adaptation. Importantly, these factors are not gender-neutral (Terry, 2009; Tschakert, van Oort, St. Clair, & LaMadrid, 2013). Similarly, national and global policies also constrain community members' access to local resources and institutions, which may also have differential gender impacts (Adhikari & Taylor, 2012). Therefore, there is a need to understand the gender-specific implications of the technological solutions to climate change, for example, geoengineering (Buck et al., 2014; Cummings & Rosenthal, 2018), GM crops (Qaim, 2010; Qaim & Kouser, 2013), among others. Just as important to study are gender-differentiated impacts of technocratic policy solutions that prescribe new technologies as easy solutions to the climate crisis. Such "managerial discourse renders invisible local experiences with climatic variability, agency, and autonomous adaptive strategies of the most vulnerable" (Tschakert & Machado, 2012, p. 277).

For example, adaptation in the agriculture sector in India needs to be understood within the larger structural changes that have taken place in recent decades, such as the liberalizing of the economy, declining subsidies for agriculture, reduced state funding in agriculture research, and increased role of transnational corporations (TNCs) in the agriculture sector. For example, India is witnessing agrarian crises including increased suicide rates by farmers, often from low-income households (Anderson & Genicot, 2015; Gruère & Sengupta, 2011; Mohanty, 2005; Sainath, 2013); low productivity; increased large-scale migration of agriculture laborers (Reddy & Mishra, 2009); and increased costs of pesticides and seeds (see Patnaik, Moyo, & Shivji, 2011; Reddy & Mishra, 2009). Official records showed that a farmer commits suicide every half hour in India, with suicide rates among Indian farmers in 2011 being 47% higher than the rest of the population (Sainath, 2013). Women farmer suicides, however, are not categorized as *farmer* suicides. This is because a farmer is considered as someone who owns land, and in India, the male head of household is often the only legally registered owner of the land (Sainath, 2009).

Compounding this trend, the specific needs and challenges of marginal and poor farmers are not addressed in government policies on climate change and agriculture development (see Byravan & Rajan, 2012), such as the 100-day work guarantee program. The government runs a 100-day work guarantee scheme in rural areas where citizens are entitled to demand government for work for 100 days in a year. A variety of projects to improve soil fertility, build check dams, repair roads, harvest water, and other development work are funded thereby providing local employment, particularly during the summer months when there is a lack of agriculture work. While these programs are aimed to help increase adaptive capacity, they also reinforce existing gender inequities in access and benefits of the program (Das, 2013; Gupta, 2009; Narayanan, 2008). For example, women face several social barriers for equal participation, particularly with low level of participation from the most disadvantaged sections of society; for example, only

17% of workers in the scheme were from lower castes, otherwise framed to be primary beneficiaries (Khera & Nayak, 2009).

In this backdrop, some of the key questions this chapter seeks to answer are: (1) how do poor women farmers talk about adaptation in the agriculture sector and (2) what are the alternative strategies of development and climate change adaptation as practiced and voiced by women farmers? This chapter presents the findings of a research project, which focused on one marginalized group, namely women farmers from low-income households belonging to lower caste communities.

Method

This project was carried out in and around Zaheerabad Mandal, Andhra Pradesh, located about 100 kilometers from the state capital city of Hyderabad. It recruited women farmers belonging to Deccan Development Society (DDS) sanghams, which are voluntary village-level associations of women farmers from low-income households.

Study site

The DDS is a three-decade-old grassroots organization working in about 75 villages with women's sanghams consisting of over 5,000 women members in the Medak district of Andhra Pradesh. Most of the women farmers work primarily as agriculture laborers and are able to lease and later own small tracts of land with the help of loans from their sanghams. Many continue this work to supplement their incomes. The basic principle of DDS is to support autonomous communities, where community members have access to and control over food production, seed, natural resources, market, and media. Several initiatives have been launched by the women farmers, including, for example, establishing a seed bank and providing agricultural loans to groups of women farmers. In addition to storing seeds, the seed bank also loans seeds to its members, and members can repay the loan in seeds. In 1996, sangham members designed and managed an alternative public distribution system (PDS) that emphasized local production and supply of grains. The PDS is a government-run scheme that provides subsidized food to low-income households. The government-run PDS relies primarily on wheat and rice distribution, often procured from regions throughout India with high levels of irrigation and distributed across India (DDS, 2004). The sangham members also organize an annual biodiversity festival, where women farmers travel to different villages alongside the seed carts, emphasizing the importance of seed and food sovereignty.

Moreover, identifying a need to communicate and articulate their concerns, women farmers have also participated in creating a community media space. The first community radio in India was started by a DDS sangham in 1998, with support from UNESCO (see Pavarala & Malik, 2007). Similarly, the women farmers have also become documentary filmmakers with several titles to their credit. Two documentaries that have received wide viewership are *Bt Cotton in Warangal: A three year fraud* and *Why are Warangal Farmers Angry with Bt Cotton*. These documentaries critically reflect on the impact of shifting to Bt cotton cultivation on poor farmers. The latter was translated into several languages, including French, Spanish, Thai, and German.

Data collection and analysis

This project conducted three focus groups and 25 in-depth interviews. The focus groups each had four to six women famers affiliated with DDS sanghams and lasted about 40–60 minutes. The discussions were conducted in the local language, Telugu, and took place in the DDS office in Pastapura and the nearby villages, Metalkunta and Yedakkulapalli. Most of the in-depth interviews were conducted in the DDS office in Pastapur. All the participants belonged to the low caste in India, the Dalit. They ranged in age from about 40 years to about 60 years and were members of DDS sanghams.

The key difference between the current participatory research method and standard qualitative research methods is opening the discursive spaces of what constitutes "climate change" and the key barriers and opportunities to solve the climate change problem. The researchers reflexively engaged with their academic training and position that tends to promote a unidimensional "scientific expertise." Finally, the researchers checked with the participants if they completely and accurately captured the expressed concerns.

Open-ended questions asked about perceptions about changing weather patterns, perceived causes of changes, perceived effects of changing weather patterns on agriculture practices, extant adaptation strategies, and promising adaptation solutions. The interviews were translated into English and transcribed. Translating interviews from Telugu to English was difficult, and the researchers reviewed all interview content to ensure accuracy.

The next stage involved coding the transcripts sentence by sentence, following the open coding process as described by Strauss and Corbin (1997). The open codes were descriptive in nature, or coded from the words used by the interviewees. Next, the open codes were further categorized under different themes. For example, open codes such as "rainfall has decreased," "uncertainty about monsoon onset," "rainfall at inappropriate times," and "not enough rains now" were coded under the theme, *perceptions about changing weather patterns.* Open codes such as "rainfall and crop choices," "confidence to grow some food crops even in less rainfall," and "some crops tolerate more rain, and some can grow in less rain" were categorized under the theme, *current adaptation response.* In addition to those two themes, the researchers identified a third theme, *adaptation policies that they seek to implement at the local, state, and national government levels.* Discussion of those themes foregrounds listening as an entry point to underscoring gender in climate change discussions and policymaking processes.

Results

Perceptions about changing rainfall patterns and its impacts

Women farmers reported several changes in their local weather patterns over the past ten years, including decreasing rainfall patterns, increasing uncertainty in predictability of monsoons, and the associated impacts on agriculture yields. Their perceptions of weather patterns were articulated through comparison with previous experiences, particularly giving examples from agricultural fields. For example, in a focus group interview in Metalkunta village, Radhamman (all names changed to ensure participants' anonymity) stated,

> Because, ten years ago, the rainy season used to be for a longer duration, and not like now-a-days. Ten years ago, if it rained for two to three months, the soil used to get muddy. Although our soil is hard and dry, and we won't be able to walk. . . . When it rains now, it is merely a sprinkle. . . . We are just able to see two or three heavy rains in the period of four months of the rainy season. There are no heavy rains anymore.

Other members in the focus group agreed that that the summer season has increased in duration, while the rainfall season duration has decreased. Moreover, they added that it had become increasingly difficult to predict when it would rain. This increased unpredictability of rainfall had increased uncertainty about the sowing season. According to Varsamma,

> . . . it is not raining at the scheduled times. It rains only once in a while. Because of this, many people are not sure about when to sow seeds. People here plant during monsoon season. It's a tradition. But if it does not rain, when will we plan to sow? So some people, whatever may happen, believing in God's goodwill, will sow, hoping it will rain sometime. So other people think that it has been 15 days and still no

rains, and they are not sure about the yields. Some other people only sow after it rains. But people feel that the crop may not result in good yields if it is planted after the season. So we observe some changes in the cropping patterns.

This increasing uncertainty in rainfall also results in other changes; for example, according to Varsamma, changing rainfall patterns have also affected pest cycles, as pests seem to infest the crops at irregular times. In these ways, women farmers recount their experiences with changing rainfall patterns. It appears that the women farmers perceive increasing uncertainty and a complex relationship between rainfall patterns, sowing time, pest cycles, and crop yields.

Adaptation to unpredictable rainfall patterns

Women farmers reported several adaptation steps they undertake to deal with changing rainfall patterns. Participants mentioned that one of the ways they have adapted to shifting rainfall patterns is to grow several varieties of food crops suitable to the region, some of which can grow with less water, while other crops can withstand heavy rainfall. According to Sukamma,

> If we plant rice, we need more rain, and more water. If we plant pearl millet that requires very less water, even if there is less rainfall, we can still harvest some crops. We are confident that the kind of crops we grow can tolerate low rainfall. We have hard soil here, so sorghum and pearl millet suits this region. Even if it rains more, some crops such as sorghum does not give good yields. Redgram crop needs more water. So some crops can tolerate more rain, and others, less rain. So when we plant these varieties of crops, we can expect at least get two bags when it rains less than usual, instead of four bags for normal rainfall. If we plant only crops that require more water, we may not have any yields.

Growing these varieties of crops, on their small tracts of land they own or lease, appears to be an important adaptation strategy to manage increasing uncertainty in rainfall patterns. Women farmers also mentioned that the increased diversity in food crops has an additional benefit of increasing biodiversity in their farms and in the region, as well as providing different varieties of nutrition for their families. According to Anjamma, "The benefit is that now we will have four varieties of crops, four varieties of food, four varieties of seeds, four varieties of animal feed." In other words, not only do women farmers report a variety of changes in the weather patterns, but report several adaptation steps they undertake. These responses – such as planting a variety of crops – not only help them adapt to varying rainfall patterns but also ensure a diversity of food for families and ecological bio-diversity in the farms and villages.

Women, agriculture practices, and adaptation

The adaptation actions that women farmers report earlier also reveal that several of these actions are also adaptations to socioeconomic conditions in their households and communities. For example, the choice of crops and the yields are also entwined in power relations between husband and wife. Several women farmers mentioned that access and control over farms and crops is important to preserve their access to food and good health. When asked why the relationship between land and women is important, Algol-amma mentioned,

> Why because men often go for only one kind of crop. That crop they sell it in the market. But women think in many different angles. She will think about cultivating spices for home, and they keep going to the field often. When they go to the field, they often take some goat or buffalo along with them. That way, as they go often, they get a lot of work done. So if they have relationship with land, they can do good farming.

When asked if there is any connection between women farmers and growing a variety of crops, Padayamma said that it is important because not only will women have control over the fields and their produce but also over what food they cook at home to ensure the family's nutritional requirements are met. Similarly, Sadaamma mentioned,

> Women have to wait for men to bring home food, and as such, men control the food and nourishment for the family. But if women have access to land and farming, she can farm and cook out of her choice. She can decide what to cook today and tomorrow. Otherwise she must wait for her husband to go to the market and buy food. And till that time, she has to go hungry. Otherwise she can do everything on her own, without depending on anyone.

However, if the family invests in cash crops, such as cotton or sugarcane, instead of food crops, Kistamma explained then the money will go into the hands of the husband, and she has to be dependent on him. Narrating some of the domestic conflicts over farm profits, Chinamma said,

> Sometimes, even the husband and sons question us about the money we earned. If anybody has a bad husband or son, they will beat the woman

and ask us money for consuming alcohol instead of contributing for the family. They will make the woman work and even ask money for drinking. They will warn us if we don't give the money, they won't allow us to be in the home and we have to find another place to stay.

This relationship between women and control over land and crops appears to be particularly important because women are considered responsible for food and the well-being of the family. In addition, it appears that access to land and crops has a direct impact on their ability to assert their economic sovereignty. The participants reported a gender gap in how women compared to men make choices about crops and their impact on the family's health and income, apart from relations of gender equality. These adaptation actions not only help them cope with changing rainfall patterns but are also instrumental in changing the gender power relations.

Seed and food sovereignty for successful adaptation to climate impacts

Women farmers interviewed in the study invoke their ability to exercise power over seeds and fields as a means to successful climate change adaptation. For example, one of the first programs that sangham members implemented was to provide loans to landless women farmers to rent small tracts of land to grow food crops using natural manure. Describing the shift from being agriculture laborers, who owned small tracts of uncultivable land, to becoming farmers, Rukamma mentioned:

Because at that time we did not till on our own lands. We did not have seeds. So we always used to work in rich landlords' farms as agriculture labour. So we would work all day long, and whatever we earn, come back and cook with that. But after working in DDS sangham, we feel that if I own my own field, I can grow my own crops. Why should I go and work in other people's fields? So once we started working in land we got on rent, we also felt why not grow food in our own lands. So we used to give a group of five to 15 people money to rent some land and grow crops. So what happened is that if ten people work and pay for four years, they can own the land. So all the yields that they get go to their home. So then they thought that if they work in their own fields, then there will never be shortage of food. That's the idea that came to their minds.

Similarly, opening seed banks appears to have also served an important purpose of guaranteeing access to seeds for the community. When asked about the importance of the seed bank, Chanulaamma mentioned,

It is important because earlier all the seeds used to be with Kaapulu (one of the land-owning castes in Andhra Pradesh) and obviously, an agriculture laborer like me who did not have any seeds had to rely on the owner completely. But now, with the introduction of seed banks, during rainy season, we store seeds and sow it as per our convenience.

She further mentioned that about 70 villages have their own seed banks, and she felt that seed banks have "solved the problem of scarcity of seeds for everyone, the food scarcity also has been solved and we now work in our own fields. We know the importance of working in our own fields."

Compared to earlier times when, although they had small tracts of fallow land, the farmers were not able to grow crops because they lacked access to seeds, they are now able to store different varieties of seeds with the seed bank. When asked why they do not use government seeds, Candramma was skeptical if the seeds provided by government and other private corporations were trustworthy, may require pesticide use, and if such seeds were suited to the semi-arid climatic conditions of the region. Moreover, she pointed out that accessing government seeds would require one to travel to distant places, such as to the district headquarters, and may require additional investment in the form of pesticides and fertilizers. In other words, their ability to exert agency through ownership of land, seeds, crops, and market as well as enact programs that enhance their sovereignty appear to be key to successful adaptation.

Adaptation policies that women farmers oppose and support

When asked about what kind of government policies they would support that will help them adapt, the sangham members narrated a variety of programs they conducted to voice their concerns about policies. These included mass media campaigns opposing the government and corporate promotion of GM crops as a solution to climate change and agrarian crises, running an alternative food distribution program, and more recently, demonstrating at an important climate change conference in Copenhagen. However, they also noted deep skepticism of government, including academic experts, support for policies they seek to implement.

For example, one of the issues they have been fighting for is to get the government to accept millet as part of the PDS. Critiquing the government-run PDS, Chunamma said that traditionally, rice is not a staple food in the region, as rice requires irrigation access. Moreover, the rice that the government provides is often of low quality and lacks nutritional value. As part of the alternative PDS scheme, the sangham members surveyed fallow lands that could be used for food cultivation. The beneficiaries of the PDS were identified using community consultation processes, thereby reducing the errors of excluding households who need the food most but are unable to provide proper paperwork to get government benefits. This way, the alternative PDS was found to generate employment, increase household income levels, increase agriculture productivity, and was able to address food and nutritional security. About 5,000 acres of fallow land was brought under cultivation under this program, generating 2.5 lakh person days of employment every season, and helped to feed 50,000 poor households (see DDS, 2004).

Few participants provided another example of government programs that led to unintended consequences, even though the program aims to aid climate change adaptation. For example, the government-run 100-day work guarantee scheme in rural areas aimed to help increase adaptive capacity and also reinforces existing caste and gender inequities with disproportional benefits. According to Pollamma,

> Generally, under the 100 days' work scheme, they make people work to improve agricultural land. But the government never takes up such jobs in our lands because we are poor and un-influential. Only the influential in the village get loans and get sanctions to drill bore. Such works will be done only in the lands of rich who can influence the government officers. When we went to ask, they say you are working in sangham, you people have lot of money and you are providing employment for the other people. So why don't you do it for yourself. This way they show partiality. This situation has to be changed. The relevant officers have to visit different lands, do a survey, and see which lands need attention, rather than sitting in offices and passing orders. Even our lands need to be cleaned under this work but we are not getting attention from the government officers at all. Although they do not help us better our farms, they still call us to work in other farms, in the farms of rich and influential people.

The narratives of women farmers suggest that vulnerability and successful adaptation is not only related to climate change impacts, but is situated within local contexts of food and farm access, and in the global context of increasing industrialization of agriculture practices, especially the corporate takeover of seeds and farm produce. Having access to their own farms and growing different varieties of crops that can withstand changing rainfall patterns are important adaptation measures. At the same time, adaptation measures such as work guarantee schemes often take place in the farms of rich and influential farmers; thereby, government programs are found to perpetuate the prevailing structural differences in access to resources.

Discussion

This chapter foregrounds the voices of lower caste women farmers from low-income households from a semi-arid region in south India to understand how they conceptualize the problem of climate change and what adaptation strategies they support. Women farmers not only perceive a decrease in annual rainfall patterns, but also state that the shift in rainfall patterns has affected their cropping cycles, as well as shifts in pest cycles that, in turn, affect crop yields. They are already implementing several adaptation measures to cope with decreasing rainfall patterns, such as planting a variety of food crops that can survive both low and high rainfall patterns. By doing so, they state they are able to not only preserve biodiversity in their farms and in the region, but also are able to help supply diverse nutritious food for their families. Women farmers are critical of government policies, specifically related to encouraging Bt cotton cultivation, the government's PDS scheme that does not include millet, and inequitable access to benefits from government programs such as the 100-day work guarantee scheme.

Memories of walking in hard and dry fields that turn muddy during rainfall season, increasing unpredictability in onset and duration of seasons, and simultaneously changes in pest cycles and yields are some of the ways women farmers construct climate change in this study. Previous studies have shown that members in rural communities construct climate change through their everyday lived experiences of agriculture practices and access to food (Carr, 2008; Eriksen et al., 2005; Eriksen et al., 2011). Wangui (2014) showed that pastoralist communities in Masai understand climate change through gendered livelihood impacts such as access to water, fuel, and food. These gendered experiences of what constitutes climate change are an alternative to objective, context-free, and value-laden scientific and technocratic frames of climate change.

The findings of this study indicate that women farmers believe that unless their concerns about the relationship between women and agriculture, food security, and seed sovereignty are addressed, adaptation policies will most likely hinder social change and more fundamentally continue the technology-centered social change that lies at the heart of climate change processes (e.g., Bee et al., 2013; Eriksen et al., 2011). For example, some governments and economists have argued that GM crops are an important climate change adaptation strategy, especially for poor women farmers (Glover, 2010a, 2010b; Qaim & Kouser, 2013; Zilberman, 2014). The rationale for this argument is the measured success of GM cotton in India and elsewhere. The primary concern in economic studies of GM crops focuses on profits and yields; few studies investigate the impact of GM crops on farmers' food access and security, preservation of biodiversity, and loss of indigenous knowledge systems and forms (Stone, 2010).

Women farmers' narratives show a need to move away from yield and profit oriented assessments, to a comprehensive change in gender relations in agriculture practices and power relations within a family. These assertions are supported by several empirical studies which indicate the heightened risks of GM crops for poor farmers due to their capital and resource intensive nature (Morse et al., 2012; Crost et al., 2007). For example, Stone (2010) and Glover (2010a, 2010b) showed that findings of beneficial effects of GM crops are largely biased in favor of rich farmers. In fact, studies have shown that profits from Bt cotton are contingent on several factors, including farm size, access to resources such as irrigation, and credit.

The 100-day rural work program is potentially one of the important adaptation policies in India, especially for the rural poor. Although women constitute a substantial proportion of workers participating in the 100-day rural work guarantee program, women farmers in this study reveal constraints for equal access, participation, and benefits of the program. These claims are found consistent at the national level as well as in regional studies (Das, 2013; Gupta, 2009; Narayanan, 2008). For example, although the program is credited to provide equal wages for women, women face several social barriers for equal participation, and the performance levels vary across states (Khera & Nayak, 2009). In 2012, although a majority of women were enrolled to find work, only 19% of female-headed households with no adult males reported seeking work, and only 16% actually worked. Only a minority of females from lower castes (17%), widows (17%), and females with young children (9%) reported to have worked in the program (Khera & Nayak, 2009). Narayanan (2008) pointed out that the program had no facility for childcare, which constrains the participation of young mothers.

In addition, the current study found that rich landlords and local administration officials use the "empowered" women collective trope to dismiss protests by women farmers that the benefits of the work are not equally distributed. Recently, Amaral, Bandyopadhyay, and Sensarma (2015) found that increased female labor participation following the Mahatma Gandhi National Rural Employment Guarantee Scheme (NREGS) increased instances of gender violence. Similarly, Anderson and Genicot (2015) found that a shift in property rights for women in India was associated with increased cases of domestic violence. Together, these studies suggest that social change is rarely simple or easy, and climate change and developmental policies need to explicitly address such unexpected consequences.

Disempowering discourses about "the poor victim" renders adaptive strategies of the most vulnerable either invisible (Tschakert & Machado, 2012) or used to justify technology fixes as the only suitable route for development and social change (Bee et al., 2013). Technology fixes to solve climate change, for example, the adoption of GM crops, are considered value-neutral, objective, and context-free. Moreover, adaptation is framed as doing something "new" while old cultural practices are considered not being able to cope with rapid, unanticipated impacts of climate change. Adaptation solutions that such communities propose are also dismissed as unique and not applicable to international contexts (Cameron, 2012). Such framing renders local knowledge and indigenous developed technologies outdated and in need of modernization. This study points to different ways that women farmers are already adapting to climate change risks, and the policies that may hinder their adaptive capacities. As scholars have argued, there is a need to identify social biases and discriminatory institutional practices that perpetuate unequal access and control over resources that "undermine timely, fair and successful adaptive responses" (Tschakert & Machado, 2012, p. 282).

When we asked what kind of community-academic partnership one can envision, some women farmers showed skepticism. They asked, "Will you care to listen?" Their prior experiences with advocacy showed that government, including academic experts, may notice their work, but do not listen and participate in dialogue. Climate change and development policymaking processes have often been limited within communities of experts, dominated by Western science. This has largely resulted in framing climate change as a problem that can be solved by technology fixes. A gendered analysis of climate change impacts and adaptation can resist and open discursive spaces for participation by marginalized and vulnerable poor women farmers in developing solutions to climate change. Listening and advocating the concerns of vulnerable groups can help the call of "no climate justice without gender justice" result in transformative change, grounded in the participatory agency of communities of women from the global South. When asked what it would mean to demonstrate that someone has listened to them, Ramamma said,

> The government should recommend our farming techniques and crops. Our crops could get better market rates, or in other matters, our seeds should get preference. Anyone who is doing this should get recognition. Recognition means, that you give others subsidy, we should also get subsidy and that is a forward-looking policy. Only when they do that, we will know they have listened to us.

Acknowledgements

National University of Singapore provided funding for this project. We want to thank DDS advisory board members and other community members for participating in this study. We also thank researchers at Culture-Centered Approaches to Research and Evaluation at National University of

Singapore for insightful comments and suggestions on earlier drafts of this chapter.

References

Adhikari, B., & Taylor, K. (2012). Vulnerability and adaptation to climate change: A review of local actions and national policy response. *Climate and Development, 4*(1), 54–65. doi:10.1080/17565529.2012.664958

Amaral, S., Bandyopadhyay, S., & Sensarma, R. (2015). Employment programmes for the poor and female empowerment: The effect of NREGS on gender-based violence in India. *Journal of Interdisciplinary Economics, 27*(2), 199–218. doi:10.1177/0260107915582295

Anderson, S., & Genicot, G. (2015). Suicide and property rights in India. *Journal of Development Economics, 114*, 64–78. doi:10.1016/j.jdeveco.2014.11.004

Arora-Jonsson, S. (2011). Virtue and vulnerability: Discourses on women, gender and climate change. *Global Environmental Change, 21*(2), 744–751. doi:10.1016/j.gloenvcha.2011.01.005

Bee, B., Biermann, M., & Tschakert, P. (2013). Gender, development, and rights-based approaches: Lessons for climate change adaptation and adaptive social protection. In M. Alston & K. Whittenbury (Eds.), *Research, action and policy: Addressing the gendered impacts of climate change* (pp. 95–108). Dordrecht, Netherlands: Springer.

Buck, H. J., Gammon, A. R., & Preston, C. J. (2014). Gender and geoengineering. *Hypatia, 29*(3), 651–669. doi:10.1111/hypa.12083

Byravan, S., & Rajan, S. C. (2012). *An evaluation of India's national action plan on climate change*. Retrieved from https://papers.ssrn.com/sol3/papers.cfm?abstract_id=2195819

Cameron, E. S. (2012). Securing indigenous politics: A critique of the vulnerability and adaptation approach to the human dimensions of climate change in the Canadian Arctic. *Global Environmental Change, 22*(1), 103–114. doi:10.1016/j.gloenvcha.2011.11.004

Carr, E. (2008). Between structure and agency: Livelihoods and adaptation in Ghana's central region. *Global Environmental Change, 18*, 689–699.

Crost, B., Shankar, B., Bennett, R., & Morse, S. (2007). Bias from farmer self-selection in genetically modified crop productivity estimates: Evidence from Indian data. *Journal of Agricultural Economics, 58*(1), 24–36.

Cummings, C. L., & Rosenthal, S. (2018). Climate change and technology: Examining opinion formation of geoengineering. *Environment Systems and Decisions*, 1–8. doi:10.1007/s10669-018-9683-8

Cuomo, C. J. (2011). Climate change, vulnerability, and responsibility. *Hypatia, 26*(4), 690–714. doi:10.1111/j.1527-2001.2011.01220.x

Das, U. (2013). *Does political connections and affiliation affect allocation of benefits in the rural employment guarantee scheme: Evidence from West Bengal, India*. SSRN Scholarly Paper No. ID 2262533. Rochester, NY: Social Science Research Network. Retrieved from http://papers.ssrn.com/abstract=2262533

DDS. (2004). *A study on alternative public distribution system*. Hyderabad, India. Retrieved from www.ddsindia.com/www/PDF/dds_pds%20text.pdf

Eriksen, S. H., Aldunce, P., Bahinipati, C. S., Martins, R. D. A., Molefe, J. I., Nhemachena, C., . . . & Ulsrud, K. (2011). When not every response to climate change is a good one: Identifying principles for sustainable adaptation. *Climate and Development, 3*(1), 7–20.

Eriksen, S. H., Brown, K., & Kelly, P. M. (2005). The dynamics of vulnerability: Locating coping strategies in Kenya and Tanzania. *Geographical Journal, 171*(4), 287–305. doi:10.1111/j.1475-4959.2005.00174.x

Glover, D. (2010a). Exploring the resilience of Bt cotton's 'pro-poor success story'. *Development and Change, 41*(6), 955–981. doi:10.1111/j.1467-7660.2010.01667.x

Glover, D. (2010b). The corporate shaping of GM crops as a technology for the poor. *Journal of Peasant Studies, 37*(1), 67–90. doi:10.1080/03066150903498754

Goh, A. H. (2012). *A literature review of the gender-differentiated Impacts of climate change on women's and men's assets and well-being in developing countries.* CAPRi Working Paper No. 106. Washington, DC: IFPRI. Retrieved from www.ifpri.org/sites/default/files/publications/capriwp106.pdf

Gruère, G., & Sengupta, D. (2011). Bt cotton and farmer suicides in India: An evidence-based assessment. *Journal of Development Studies, 47*(2), 316–337. doi:10.1080/00220388.2010.492863

Gupta, S. (2009). Women in India's national rural employment guarantee scheme. In S. Razavi (Ed.), *The gendered impacts of liberalization: Towards eEmbedded liberalism?* (pp. 327–356). New York, NY: Routledge.

Harding, S. (2008). *Sciences from below: Feminisms, postcolonialities, and modernities.* Durham, NC: Duke University Press.

IPCC. (n.d.). *IPCC Working Group II: Glossary.* Retrieved October 31, 2013 from www.ipcc.ch/publications_and_data/ar4/wg2/en/annexessglossary-a-d.html

Israel, A., & Sachs, C. (2013). A climate for feminist intervention: Feminist science studies and climate change. In M. Alston & K. Whittenbury (Eds.), *Research, action and policy: Addressing the gendered impacts of climate change* (pp. 33–51). Dordrecht, Netherlands: Springer.

Kakota, T., Nyariki, D., Mkwambisi, D., & Kogi-Makau, W. (2011). Gender vulnerability to climate variability and household food insecurity. *Climate and Development, 3*(4), 298–309. doi:10.1080/17565529.2011.627419

Khera, R., & Nayak, N. (2009). Women workers and perceptions of the national rural employment guarantee act. *Economic and Political Weekly, 44*(43), 49–57.

MacGregor, S. (2010). Gender and climate change: From impacts to discourses. *Journal of the Indian Ocean Region, 6*(2), 223–238. doi:10.1080/19480881.2010.536669

Mohanty, B. (2005). 'We are like the living dead': Farmer suicides in Maharashtra, Western India. *The Journal of Peasant Studies, 32*(2), 243–276. doi:10.1080/03066150500094485

Moosa, C. S., & Tuana, N. (2014). Mapping a research agenda concerning gender and climate change: A review of the literature. *Hypatia, 29*(3), 677–694. doi:10.1111/hypa.12085

Morse, S., Mannion, A. M., & Evans, C. (2012). Location, location, location: Presenting evidence for genetically modified crops. *Applied Geography, 34*, 274–280.

Narayanan, S. (2008). Employment guarantee, women's work and childcare. *Economic and Political Weekly, 43*(9), 10–13.

Patnaik, U., Moyo, S., & Shivji, I. G. (2011). *The agrarian question in the neoliberal era: Primitive accumulation and the peasantry*. Cape Town: Fahamu/Pambazuka.

Pavarala, V., & Malik, K. (2007). *Other voices: The struggle of community radio in India*. New Delhi, India: SAGE.

Qaim, M. (2010). Benefits of genetically modified crops for the poor: Household income, nutrition, and health. *New Biotechnology, 27*(5), 552–557. doi:10.1016/j.nbt.2010.07.009

Qaim, M., & Kouser, S. (2013). Genetically modified crops and food security. *PLoS ONE, 8*(6), e64879. doi:10.1371/journal.pone.0064879

Reddy, D. N., & Mishra, S. (2009). *Agrarian crisis in India*. New Delhi, India: Oxford University Press.

Rogers, E. M. (2003). *Difussion of innovations* (5th ed.). New York, NY: Free Press.

Sainath, P. (2009, December 12). The farm crisis: why have over one lakh farmers killed themselves in the past decade? Retrieved from https://psainath.org/the-farm-crisis-why-have-over-one-lakh-farmers-killed-themselves-in-the-past-decade/

Sainath, P. (2013, May 18). Farmers' suicide rates soar above the rest. *The Hindu*. Mumbai. Retrieved from www.thehindu.com/opinion/columns/sainath/farmers-suicide-rates-soar-above-the-rest/article4725101.ece

Seager, J. (2009). Death by degrees: Taking a feminist hard look at the 2 degree climate policy. *Women, Gender, and Research, 18*(3–4), 11–21.

Stone, G. D. (2010). The anthropology of genetically modified crops. *Annual Review of Anthropology, 39*(1), 381–400. doi:10.1146/annurev.anthro.012809.105058

Strauss, A. L., & Corbin, J. M. (Eds.). (1997). *Grounded theory in practice*. Thousand Oaks, CA: SAGE.

Terry, G. (2009). No climate justice without gender justice: An overview of the issues. *Gender & Development, 17*(1), 5–18. doi:10.1080/13552070802696839

Tschakert, P., & Machado, M. (2012). Gender justice and rights in climate change adaptation: Opportunities and pitfalls. *Ethics and Social Welfare, 6*(3), 275–289. doi:10.1080/17496535.2012.704929

Tschakert, P., van Oort, B., St. Clair, A. L., & LaMadrid, A. (2013). Inequality and transformation analyses: A complementary lens for addressing vulnerability to climate change. *Climate and Development, 5*(4), 340–350. doi:10.1080/17565529.2013.828583

Wangui, E. E. (2014). Gender, livelihoods and the construction of climate change among Masai pastoralists. In A. M. Oberhauser & I. Johnston-Anumonwo (Eds.), *Global perspectives on gender and space: Engaging feminism and development* (pp. 163–180). New York, NY: Routledge.

Zilberman, D. (2014). IPCC AR5 overlooked the potential of unleashing agricultural biotechnology to combat climate change and poverty. *Global Change Biology, 21*(2), 501–503. doi:10.1111/gcb.12765

Index

Numbers in italics denote figures.

Printed in Great Britain
by Amazon

35781559R00075